Manufactured by Amazon.ca
Bolton, ON

21752560R00085

About the Author

Sunita Osborn, Psy.D., M.A., is a writer and licensed psychologist practicing in Houston, Texas who works with adults and couples. After finding herself lost and without a map after her own experiences of pregnancy loss, she is committed to helping women cope with the pain of miscarriage, increasing awareness and decreasing stigma towards miscarriage, and promoting open dialogue on the realities of this prevalent and devastating concern.

The Miscarriage Map
What to Expect When You are No Longer Expecting

By

Dr. Sunita Osborn

The Miscarriage Map

Dedication

to my husband Michael

When I told you I wanted to write a book, you responded with such excitement and support that I believed I could write all the books in the world. Thank you for unwaveringly supporting me, listening to all the many things I have to say, and answering all my hypothetical questions. I'm so happy I get to do life with you. Also, thanks for letting me write an entire book about our lives.

Table of Contents

Foreword
DON'T SKIP THIS!

I was such a dick at my best friends' joint baby shower. I'd had a miscarriage just two months earlier, and here I was having to celebrate not one, but two babies coming into the world. Don't get me wrong, I was so happy for my best friends. I've known these women for years and consider them family, but having to pretend that I loved playing the baby games and enjoyed gazing wonderingly at their pregnant bellies while my body and heart felt so heavily empty was torture.

So, I was a dick. I obnoxiously threw myself into the games, making it my mission to win each and every one so I would get that $5 gift card from Starbucks (because hey, I can have all the caffeine I want now). I made zero effort to socialize with anyone, and after receiving a few seemingly innocuous, but deeply painful questions about when it was going to be my "turn" to have a baby, I went off on this poor, unsuspecting woman about the ridiculous practice of constantly asking people to define their next life steps to strangers and acquaintances. Shockingly, she quickly exited the conversation and everyone else gave me a wide berth for the remainder of the party. So, yeah, I was a dick.

You don't know me yet, but I'm not usually a dick. Actually, quite the opposite. Most would describe me as warm, compassionate, kind, loyal, and always ready to help others. I'm basically a human golden retriever. In my work as a psychologist, I have been described by clients as accepting, open, and friendly. My appearance as an irritable and obnoxious party guest was indicative of the huge impact a miscarriage can have on your life, your body, and the way you show up for months, maybe years after. And that's what this book is about.

For those of you reading this, I'm sorry that you have a reason for picking up this book, whether it's because of your own miscarriage or because you want to understand the miscarriage of someone close to you. If you're in the former group, I also want to offer you an invitation. I want to invite you to make the space for yourself to acknowledge, to process, and to grieve your miscarriage, because it is a BIG deal. One of the most painful questions I often asked myself during the early days of my first miscarriage was, "Am I making this too big?" For myself, for all the women, partners, and people out there, I want to offer you a resounding "NO." This is a huge, hideous, terrible, painful, traumatic, and life-changing event and we deserve all the space in the world to acknowledge that.

What this Book Is

This book is written by someone who has been on both sides of the therapeutic couch. I am a licensed psychologist trained to help individuals navigate the perils of trauma and grief and then I became a client in need of help in processing my own trauma and grief. I experienced my first miscarriage in November of 2018, and my second in March of 2019. What you'll read here is a no-holds-barred, unfiltered, deeply personal story. Some of the details aren't pretty (who sabotages a baby shower?) but I share these stories in the hopes of providing some sense of normalcy and validation, to let anyone affected by miscarriage know that it is normal to feel intense waves of devastating emotions, to get real familiar crying in public places (my favorite venue for a public cry is Panera—easy access to napkins and cookies), and to absolutely *hate* anything baby-related.

Also, general disclaimer, I do use humor in this book because as Laura Ingalls Wilder said, "A good laugh overcomes more difficulties and dissipates more dark clouds than any other one thing." The intention of my humor is in no way to make light of a painful and significant subject, but again reflects my own way of coping and processing. Additionally, I am a licensed psychologist and have drawn on my education, training, and clinical experience to inform my own experiences and to shed some light on a subject that is rarely talked about but is experienced by so many. According to the National Institutes of Health, miscarriage—which is defined as the spontaneous loss of a fetus before the 20th week of pregnancy—occurs in 10 to 25% of pregnancies.[1] Even at the lower end of the estimate, that's a staggering incidence rate: 1 out of every 10 pregnancies ends in miscarriage. With something so common, why aren't we speaking about this more? This book is my contribution to the conversation, which I hope will be ongoing.

What this Book Isn't

While this book does draw upon my education and training and is informed by research, it is not an academic text. It does not provide the answers to all the questions regarding miscarriage. The experience of a miscarriage can vary widely based on so many factors, including biological, socioeconomical, and cultural background. My experience in no way serves as representative of all women who have experienced a miscarriage, and this book does not span all the many issues that a miscarriage can impact, such as what miscarriage is like with children already in the household. It does not cover some of the specific issues a couple that identifies as LGBTQI would

---

[1] MedlinePlus. "Miscarriage." Medlineplus.gov. https://medlineplus.gov/ency/article/001488.htm (accessed May 31, 2019).

face when experiencing a miscarriage (though that is very needed and would be an awesome book). Additionally, this book does not consider the religious or spiritual impact of a miscarriage. There are some beautiful books out there that explore the religious journey following a miscarriage, but that wasn't part of my story, so this book is not one of them.

Why I Wrote This

The day I found out about my first miscarriage, I was in such a fog. I felt so consumed by sadness, anger, and grief that I didn't know if I would ever come out of it. I needed a map, some type of guide for how to manage this new hell I was in. As we all know, miscarriage is a topic that touches so many, but is so rarely discussed. I scoured the web, but nothing I found seemed like exactly what I needed. I wanted a guide that was not religiously based and could provide me with another woman's journey, coupled with research-based insights to help me understand what I was walking through and where I needed to go next. When I couldn't find this, I started writing. I began by writing my personal story, the immediate events and the emotions I was experiencing, and then continued to write as I explored the various hurdles in my journey, including the impact of pregnancy loss on my relationship, the shame associated with miscarriage, and the unpalatable but undeniable anger I felt towards pregnant people and all things baby-related. Thus, *The Miscarriage Map* was born. The book is dedicated to providing women and their loved ones with the map they need to traverse the painful, shocking, and all-encompassing journey that is a miscarriage.

Chapter 1

WELL, THAT DIDN'T GO EXACTLY AS PLANNED

I still remember the exact moment I realized I was ready to have kids. My husband Michael and I were driving to Lake Charles, Louisiana to visit the casinos for his 30th birthday on July 5th 2018 – his idea of fun, not mine. I was behind the wheel, reflecting on how happy I was about our recent move back to my hometown of Houston, our beautiful house, my fulfilling new job, and what a great place our relationship was in, and it hit it me so clearly: "I'm ready to have kids!" I have only had a few things hit me with such certainty and clarity – wanting to be a psychologist was one, deciding to take a chance on my husband in that shady line dancing bar in Indianapolis was another. And there in that car, barreling down I-10, I experienced another moment of absolute certainty in which I knew I was ready to take this next step in my life.

Fast forward a few months. After a lot of discussions, heart-to-hearts, and weighing all the logistical, emotional, and relationship factors, we decided we were ready (in other words Michael could have waited a few more months, but I was very ready). I went off my birth control pills in September and immediately went all in on the act of trying to become pregnant.

I would love to have been one of those women who just "had fun" and let things happen naturally, and my husband certainly wished for that. But alas, I don't roll that way. I'm a bit of a control freak and love a good plan more than I love a basket full of puppies. Some of y'all may have been down this neurotic baby-making path before, and let me tell you, it can quickly consume you. I researched and bought the ovulation predictor kits and started tracking and recording the results. I bought the special pre-seed lube that was guaranteed to increase our chances of conception. As you can imagine, a bottle of lubricant featuring a picture of a pregnant woman and the label "Pre-seed lube: Help your chances of conception" in huge font can be a real mood-killer. However, I was willing to make that sacrifice, and spent so much time and energy tracking everything and anything that was possibly trackable, like I was planning for world domination, because I wanted a baby that badly.

All that obsessing paid off (thank you, slightly concerning neuroticism), and I found out I was pregnant on September 27th. When I saw that blue positive sign, my reaction was straight out of a happy, rosy movie. I jumped up and down and silent-screamed—Michael was still asleep—and then lunged for the mirror, inspecting myself for immediate signs of pregnancy. I remember thinking "This is happening! This is where it all starts." I had always thoughts I would be one of those people who meticulously and thoughtfully planned a creative way to tell their partner about their pregnancy, but I am the least creative person in the world, and I couldn't contain my excitement. So, as soon as my husband woke up, he found me creepily sitting next to him on the bed, where I'd been staring at him, waiting for the first sign of movement. Then I said for the first time in my life, "We are going to be parents!" Michael immediately sat up and hugged me. He asked me how I felt and before we could really savor the moment, I jumped into planning mode and called my gynecologist who was also an OB to schedule an appointment. I was already so excited to get those hallowed ultrasound photos I had seen others proudly share and get a first glimpse of our baby.

My gyno—and now OB!—scheduled our first

appointment for October 2nd and in hindsight, I'm surprised she allowed me to come in that early, as my last period had been August 22nd. But at that moment, such thoughts weren't anywhere on my radar. All I could think of was my ecstatic excitement—and that it seemed like October 2nd would never get here.

When I finally arrived at the office, my OB hugged me and said congratulations and gave us the fun, colorful handouts all newly expecting couples receive. She had to do a transvaginal ultrasound because I was so early, and was able to point out a tiny gestational sac and not much else. The ultrasound showed the embryo's development wasn't quite as far along as my OB would expect given my last period, but she assured me that I could just be a little off on my dates, or maybe I'd ovulated later this cycle.

After this appointment, I clearly remember the disparity between my husband's reactions and mine: Michael was so excited, with no concerns whatsoever, while I immediately went into catastrophizing. As I mentioned previously, I had been tracking my ovulation meticulously, so I worried that this discrepancy in my dates meant something more. I reminded myself that I was not the doctor here and tried to focus on my OB's confidence and her assurances that everything was okay.

My doctor recommended we come back two days later to do another ultrasound and get my human chorionic gonadotropin (hCG) levels checked. hCG is a hormone normally produced by the placenta. Blood or urine tests measuring hCG levels are used to check how well your pregnancy is progressing, including your baby's development. We came back two days later as requested and were given the same news. While my hCG levels were rising appropriately, the embryo's development was still not showing quite as far along as my doctor would expect.

This is when we entered what I would call the pregnancy version of Dante's stages of hell. For the entire month of October, we were going to my OB's at least once if not twice a week. My OB assured us that we would only need to come this frequently until we were able to see a heartbeat, which would be one of the signs that this was a viable pregnancy. Previous to my experience with miscarriage, I had never thought of pregnancies in terms of viability. Naively, I believed pregnancy equaled baby. It was that simple. The month of October proved that was not the case. With each appointment, I was getting poked and prodded, a blood draw here, a transvaginal ultrasound there. For those of you who have not had this singular experience, imagine getting a fairly large probe inserted inside of you on a weekly basis by a kindly man who resembles your grandfather.

The most frustrating part was that with each appointment we were given the same news in different words every single time: "You must be really early. Everything looks normal so far. This just must be an early pregnancy. I'm not worried." Damn, how I wished I could have that luxury. I left every appointment feeling more worried than the next, and prepared for each subsequent appointment with the now familiar feelings of dread, fear, anticipation, and the tiniest bit of hope that maybe we would finally detect a little heartbeat on the ultrasound this time.

As a psychologist, it's an interesting experience being faced with anxiety. I can recognize all the fallacies in my thinking and can name about a dozen ways to respond to these thoughts. Sometimes these interventions worked, but most of the time I was just riddled by constant questions going through my head. Why was the sac so small? What could this mean? What if I should have waited a little longer to be off birth control before we started trying, like some of the sites recommended? When all these incessant questions popped into my mind, I turned to anxiety's best friend, Google. And, man, Google was quite the double-edged sword, with some sites saying all was likely well and that each pregnancy looks different, while other sites dispassionately informed me that some of the symptoms I was experiencing could be early signs of a miscarriage.

Even in the midst of anxiety as I traversed these sites, I noticed the phenomenon of confirmation bias taking over.[2] In other words, I was selectively paying attention to the information that confirmed my beliefs, which varied wildly based on my current mood. If I was riddled with "what if" questions after an appointment, I would selectively search for information that confirmed my greatest fears. "Oh god, that pain in my back could be a sign of my miscarriage." Or, "I feel like I should have thrown up by now. What could this mean?" Or, if I was preparing for my next appointment and wanted to remain hopeful for my husband, my little growing baby, and my own sanity, I would turn towards information that confirmed that "Hey, it's okay if you see no baby after a month of ultrasounds. All pregnancies are different!" I stuck onto that mantra like it was my last prayer.

Finally, we went to an appointment on November 2nd when I was supposed to be at 11 weeks, and the OB did my 500th ultrasound. The second the picture came on the screen, I knew. I had spent enough time with my old friend, Google, to know what an ultrasound at 11 weeks should look like. The sac was completely empty. The next two minutes felt like slow motion. I remember the doctor saying it looked like I was showing the signs of a miscarriage and

---

[2] Aue, Tatjana, and Hadas Okon-Singer, "Expectancy Biases in Fear and Anxiety and Their Link to Biases in Attention." Clinical Psychology Review no. 42 (2015): 83-95.

I recall the feeling of complete surrealism as my worst fears were realized. It's quite a disorienting feeling to have the nightmare you pictured so many times actually coming to life. But most of all, I remember the look on Michael's face, a look of utter sadness and devastation I had never seen before.

The doctor left the room for me to get dressed and Michael just held me while I cried. I remember crying so much as we were leaving that I could barely see straight. While Michael went to get the car, an administrative staff member pulled me into her office and asked if I was ready to start filling out the financial paperwork for my labor and delivery. "I'm having a miscarriage!" I croaked out, and broke down even further. She was taken aback and appeared confused at my reaction (surprising given where she worked), and she apologized for her mistake and said she was sorry for my loss. This was the first of many times I would hear that phrase.

I called my parents, my sister, and my best friend to tell them the news. Each call was filled with so much crying and pain that I could barely get the words out. Over the span of two minutes I considered if I should still go to work, and then rejected that idea as I couldn't stop crying, so clearly I was not in a place where I could serve my clients. I called my boss and tearfully relayed the news yet again, and she quickly told me not to worry about anything related to work. She would take care of everything and I was to contact her if I needed anything. Big sigh of relief there.

My husband jokingly refers to my family as a "caravan family" because anytime something significant happens to any of us, we all get in one car and rush over to wherever the family-member-in-need is. We've done this for car accidents, broken limbs, and crises of all magnitudes, and this time was no different. When I called with my terrible news, every one of my family members left their jobs in the middle of the day, citing a family emergency, and caravanned their way to our house. While I so appreciated my family being there, I found myself putting on a brave face for them, speaking matter-of-factly about the details of the appointments and next steps, and making jokes when I sensed they had no idea what to say to me. The thing about my family is that they are the most loyal, compassionate, and warm people ever (we really are a pack of golden retrievers), but we don't respond emotionally to each other in times of crisis. And knowing that about my family, I didn't express my needs and I made sure to not be too emotional because then, on top of being devastated, I would be sitting with my family's discomfort with my devastation.

Consequently, I was happy to have them there, to feel their support, and for them to do what they did best—show up and bring me fajitas from my favorite Mexican restaurant. But it was only after they left that I truly allowed myself to break down and feel the depths of my emotions. I cried and cried and cried. I cried like I have never cried before, with such despair and hopelessness that I truly couldn't imagine ever feeling better. I was also angry, angry that this had happened to us, angry that I had to go on functioning like a normal adult, and angry that this nightmare still wasn't over. I still had to get surgery tomorrow, and then, even though I knew it was not helpful to burden myself with the thoughts of subsequent pregnancies, I became furious thinking that I would again have to begin the laborious tracking process to become pregnant and then I would inevitably be faced with a world of anxiety even if I was able to get pregnant a second time. From every perspective I looked, my future felt overwhelming and terrifying.

There's no tidy ending to this story. No epiphany where I suddenly realize there is hope at the end of the rainbow that casts everything in a rose-colored glow. There's no ending because my story was just beginning. I had just received the news and was in a state of shock and devastation, and I still had such a ways to go.

Part II

When I wrote this first chapter following my first miscarriage, I never anticipated writing an addendum to this section. I hoped that I would have my miscarriage, gracefully process and manage the devastation and grief, and then share the redemption story that would be my next successful pregnancy. Because surely life could not be so cruel that I would go through this pain again, surely my first miscarriage had just been a fluke, just a bad roll of the genetic dice. But it looks as if the words from my last paragraph above were prophetic. My first miscarriage was just the beginning of my story, and I had such a ways to go.

Because, dear reader, I found out at the end of January 2019 that I was pregnant again. For reference, I had learned of my first pregnancy in September 2018, and then found out about the miscarriage and had a dilation and curettage (D&C) surgery in November 2018. Now here we were, just two months later, pregnant again.

My experience of pregnancy the second time around was drastically different right from the beginning. The first time I held a positive pregnancy test in my hand, I jumped up and down and was immediately filled with exhilarating joy. The second time around, my reaction was more complicated. There was joy, but there was also anxiety, shock, and just the tiniest bit of hope. I remember saying out loud, "No way, no way, no way." Actually, it was more like, "No fucking way. No fucking way. You're fucking kidding me!" My internal voice has quite the potty mouth.

My husband and I hadn't really been trying, but at the same time we weren't really doing anything to prevent pregnancy either. I know there was this little part of me that I didn't want to acknowledge that cautiously hoped if I got pregnant relatively soon after our first miscarriage, our pain and grief would just wash away and we could focus on our future with this new pregnancy. And indeed there was some truth to that. Being newly pregnant almost felt like being in a new relationship after a painful breakup. What's that charming phrase? "You have to get under someone to get over someone?" Well, I was hoping the pregnancy equivalent of that priceless adage would somehow cover up all the memories I had of the last painful months.

As it turns out, I was temporarily distracted from my grief, but that grief was replaced by an overwhelming amount of anxiety. I constantly wondered if I was going to miscarry again. It didn't help that I'd had zero symptoms before my previous miscarriage, no warning to alert me to the possibility of danger and to prepare me for the physical and emotional devastation I would soon face. During what felt like an endless wait for our first appointment, I attempted to use what I learned from my first miscarriage to manage my anxiety, relying on a combination of avoidance, distraction, and self-compassion. Michael was fantastic and never brushed off my anxieties, giving me space to share them while also reinforcing that we would make it through whatever happened.

Finally the last day of February arrived, which was when, based on the date of my last period, I would have been approximately 10 weeks. The same doctor who diagnosed my ultrasound and performed my D&C performed this ultrasound, and immediately informed us that she was seeing everything she needed to see. Our baby was measuring a little behind at 8 weeks and 6 days, but she wasn't concerned, postulating that I likely ovulated late. We were able to hear the heartbeat and I remember saying over and over, "I can't believe it. I can't believe it. I can't believe it!" as my husband and I smiled so widely at each other with such joy that our faces ached.

After that ultrasound, I released a breath that I did not realize I had been holding for the last month. All my anxieties and worries just whooshed out of me as Dr. Google informed me that a chance of miscarriage after a heartbeat is detected at close to 9 weeks is 1.5%. 1.5%! That was nothing! There was a 98.5% chance we were having this baby – I would gamble my life on those odds. For the first time in both my pregnancies, I finally felt like I could be excited and truly celebrate and acknowledge that we were having a baby. I could daydream with my husband, and we took turns picking and vetoing names. We had already told our immediate families and close friends, and we ecstatically shared our ultrasound pictures and heartbeat video with them. I finally was able to hold that hallowed ultrasound picture in my hand. We had three weeks until our next appointment and for every day leading up to it, I would look at that ultrasound, marveling at how big our baby already looked with her developing arms, and I would listen to the recording of that heartbeat with such wonder. It felt like such a privilege to hear it, that unearthly whoosh-whoosh-whoosh that testified our baby was there and thriving.

We arrived at our second appointment three weeks later in a completely different mental state than we ever had before. By now, OB appointments were associated with dread, anxiety, anticipation, and the tiniest bit of hope. I was usually feeling so worried that I could barely keep up small talk with our friendly nurse as I stared stoically ahead at the numerous happy baby photos posted on the wall before me. After our last successful appointment, I was ready to be on the excited, happy train. I imagine Michael and I seemed like a completely different couple as we laughed and joked with our nurse and commented on how adorable all those great baby photos were! We began discussing anatomy appointments at 20 weeks and what the schedule of appointments would be following this ultrasound with a sense of hopefulness and optimism.

But almost immediately after our doctor inserted the transvaginal ultrasound, I knew something was wrong: I had our last ultrasound imprinted on my mind, and the picture I was seeing now looked exactly like that, minus that beautiful, little flickering heartbeat. One glance at the doctor's face revealed her worry, and in a few seconds, she echoed my worst fears, stating that she was concerned by what she was seeing and that there was no cardiac activity. She said that she would expect the baby to be closer to 11 weeks at this point, but she looked closer to 9 weeks. I immediately started sobbing, my legs shaking as I lay exposed in the stirrups. My doctor squeezed my leg, then had another doctor confirm the diagnosis. The other doctor looked at the screen and quickly confirmed, yes, I was having another miscarriage.

We learned that day that our baby had stopped developing shortly after our last appointment. Her little heart had stopped beating. Our doctor recommended that we schedule a D&C for the next day and informed us that because I was so far along, they could get testing done on the fetal tissue to start trying to get us some answers for why we had miscarried again. She began rattling off additional tests for us to pursue, as well as a referral to an infertility specialist. An infertility specialist? That word hurt and shocked me. We had gotten pregnant twice on our own, and so quickly. We were so young, why did we need an infertility specialist? I let those questions go unanswered as I succumbed to my grief.

It feels important to acknowledge the jarring impact

that comes in the aftershocks of hearing you've had a miscarriage. After receiving that devastating news, all you may want to do is crawl into your bed and hide under the covers as the grim reality of your grief settles in around you. Every fiber of my being certainly urged me to do that. Instead, you are given no reprieve. Within mere minutes of hearing the news of our second miscarriage, we were scheduling a D&C for the next day, receiving referrals for other doctors and more appointments, and that was even before we had left the room.

Michael and I hugged and cried together as our doctor left to begin preparations for the next steps. We then made the painfully familiar journey to the hospital next door to complete our pre-op for my surgery the next day. I cried continuously as I filled out paperwork, as I got my blood drawn, as I was informed again of the procedure I would have the next day. A procedure I'd just had four months ago. I wanted to scream at them to stop telling me about this surgery. I had just been through it. I knew what it entailed to have the remains of my baby surgically removed from me. But I didn't say any of that. Instead, I nodded at all the right times, answered all the questions, and steadily let tears fall down my face, letting Michael wipe them away with a tissue.

All of the hospital staff were respectful and kind towards my consistent sobbing. One administrative assistant said, "I'm sorry. I know how you feel. I've had three or four myself." While I appreciated the sentiment and told her so, I immediately wondered, first, "Three or four"—how do you not remember each painful loss? How is that number not cemented indelibly in your brain? And second, Will that be my story one day? Will I share my story of having "three or four" losses with others? Maybe. There were no signs for me to grab hold to that would allow me to feel hopeful about the future.

Similar to our pre-op, the D&C was eerily familiar. The surgery itself went as expected with no complications, but the painful realization that I was again no longer pregnant and would not be pregnant anytime soon struck me with devastating force. While the literal experiences were relatively similar, my second experience of a miscarriage was shocking in its quickness and finality. I had woken up on a Tuesday thinking I was going to see our baby at 11 weeks and get to hear her little heartbeat again, but instead, by Wednesday I was checked into the hospital for a D&C, and by Thursday, my womb was once again acutely empty. Though there was some relief in not having to enter a state of limbo and numerous appointments where I was left with a little bit of hope and lots of anxiety, I felt like I had no time to say goodbye or come to terms with our loss. I spent the days after in a state of numbness and shock that my husband and I were in this position again.

Similar to my first experience of miscarriage, I have no tidy ending to this story. While I cling to hopes for our future, until then I am left with processing and walking through the mourning of another devastating loss. In many ways, as I'm sure you know, dear readers, this is just the beginning of our journey together.

Chapter 2

ALL THE THINGS THEY NEVER TOLD YOU: THE NITTY-GRITTY

As we begin this journey, let's talk about what we are walking into. This section is not for the faint of heart, but for the folks out there who, like me, wanted to know all the nitty-gritty details of what to expect when you are no longer expecting. So you found out you are having a miscarriage. It's terrible, it's a nightmare. Believe, me I know. But the fun does not stop there! Nope, it's not like detecting strep where they stick something in you and move it around (well, that part is true) and then can say definitively, yup, here are some antibiotics and you are good to go.

There can definitely be some variations, but in many cases, they require you to go get your blood drawn, repeatedly, get another invasive ultrasound, and then walk around in a hideous sort of limbo. Even if you have already had the miscarriage at home, you still often have to enter the miserable post-miscarriage routine of doctor's appointment, invasive tests, more doctor's appointments, rinse and repeat. Alternatively, there are the cases like me, who found out we were going to have a miscarriage, but the miscarriage process hadn't actually started yet. You then enter another type of hellish limbo where you have all the lovely symptoms of pregnancy while also carrying around the knowledge that there is no longer a growing baby inside you.

Let's just pause on that for a second, folks. Imagine if you will, that you have been told you are likely having a miscarriage but you now need to wait around for the next week doing a bunch of painful tests and waiting for results, all while having normal pregnancy symptoms such as nausea, sore breasts, and, oh wait for the best part, you STILL can't drink yet. My experience of this hellish variety of limbo occurred with my first miscarriage: I found out on a Wednesday I was likely having a miscarriage, but that needed to be confirmed by hCG tests and a repeat ultrasound the following Tuesday.

For those six days, I alternated between devastation, hope, anger, sadness, confusion, and right back to devastation again. Based on what my doctor said I knew it was extremely unlikely that there was any hope left that we would still be having a baby, but going back to my personal advisor Dr. Google, there were so many stories of women who had gone through painful journeys like mine and it turned out their baby was fine, so maybe, just maybe, we would be okay too. Obviously, we were not, and I would count that week of limbo as probably the most painful of both my miscarriage experiences. (I will share what got me through those difficult days in the next chapter.)

Hell Can Take Various Forms

While I won't be able to describe every type of miscarriage, it seems worth noting that there are many different forms a miscarriage can take and that they can occur at any point during the pregnancy. No matter how or when they occur, each do come with their own unique brand of challenges and pain. For example, a chemical pregnancy refers to a miscarriage that occurs very early, usually before five weeks, and may coincide with the time of a woman's period, making it go undetectable by some. The term "chemical pregnancy" has served as a source of distress as some feel it can question the validity of a woman actually being pregnant and experiencing a miscarriage. A blighted ovum, my first miscarriage, is a miscarriage in which the baby doesn't develop but a gestational sac continues to grow, and you may continue to experience pregnancy symptoms. I've mentioned this before, but it really is a new level of torture experiencing the symptoms of pregnancy while knowing there is no baby developing. An ectopic pregnancy occurs when a fertilized egg implants someplace other than in the uterus, such as in one of the fallopian tubes. This type of miscarriage can be particularly dangerous if the pregnancy causes the fallopian tube to burst.[3] See what I mean about different brands of torture? This is by no means an exhaustive list of the different types of miscarriage but is meant to acknowledge the unique and painful challenges we may face on our journey through pregnancy loss.

Now, after being given soul-crushing news you may (depending on the specifics of your miscarriage) be given the options of A) passing your miscarriage naturally (i.e., waiting for your miscarriage to spontaneously happen, B) taking medication to induce a miscarriage, or C) doing a dilation and curettage (D&C). Real Sophie's choice here. Now, in some cases, medical circumstances such as bleeding, infection, and/or how far along you are may dictate which option you ultimately choose. I think we can agree they're all pretty terrible and certainly have their own unique challenges and pains. We went with the D&C because that's what our doctor recommended, but let's explore the other options.

Option A: Expectant Management

Waiting for a miscarriage without intervention is an approach that doctors call "expectant management" and

---

[3] Agenor, Angena, and Sohinee Bhattacharya, "Infertility and Miscarriage: Common Pathways in Manifestation and Management," *Women's Health* no. 11.4 (2015): 527-541.

what many women call a "natural miscarriage." Some may choose this option because they would prefer to avoid medical intervention, miscarry in the privacy of their own home, and—let's get real here—avoid having to pay the significant medical bills that come with choosing the other options. Studies suggest that 80 percent of women who wait for a natural miscarriage will be able to do so without unexpected complications. This assumes that a woman is able to and willing to wait enough time to pass the fetal tissue (up to 8 weeks).[4]

There is a minor risk of hemorrhage and/or infection, but the risk is similar with a D&C. One of the challenging parts of Option A is that some women who choose natural miscarriage may end up needing or wanting a D&C later if the tissue from the pregnancy does not leave the uterus in a reasonable amount of time (i.e., up to 8 weeks).

What to expect physically depends on how early in the pregnancy the miscarriage occurred, and each woman may experience symptoms differently. There will likely be cramps and clotting, and some women may pass recognizable fetal tissue such as the gestational sac or a partially developed embryo. It may be helpful to retain some of this tissue and bring it to your doctor if you are interested in testing. Some women have described experiencing "labor pains" before experiencing their miscarriage, and I have heard many mention they were not prepared for the physical and emotional pain they endured in having a natural miscarriage. Others have shared that experiencing such a viscerally physical reaction allowed them to have some sense of closure and/or honoring of their child.

The nitty-gritty here is that you may potentially be

---

[4] Martin, I., J. Sassarini, and C. Bain, "Management of Missed Miscarriage: Examining Outcomes of Expectant, Medical and Surgical Management in EPAS Setting," *BJOG-An International Journal of Obstetrics and Gynaecology* Vol. 124:S1 (2017).

walking around in a sort of limbo for weeks not knowing if you'll start bleeding through your pants while you are at work, while you are at a friend's house, or while you are out grocery shopping. I've heard many women recommend that if you go with Option A to have a fresh set of clothes with you at all times, along with some heavy-duty pads. You will likely be experiencing some pain as well, so if possible have some pain relievers ready. If you take this route, your doctor may prescribe you some painkillers. If you need them, take them. You have been through enough, and you don't need extra physical pain on top of that. Also, the heavy, painful cramps and bleeding could last for hours, and then you will likely continue bleeding and spotting for days after.

Option B: Medication Route

This option is for women who would prefer to avoid surgery, would prefer to have their miscarriage in the privacy of their own home, and do not want to wait a potentially extended period of time for the miscarriage to begin. Let's get straight to the nitty-gritty here. **How it works**: Your doctor prescribes one or more medications, usually Cytotec (misoprostol), that cause your cervix to dilate and your uterine lining to shed. This medication may be oral or vaginal (eek), depending on the specifics of your miscarriage. You will likely be prescribed some pain medications, which again I highly recommend if you need them because you have been through enough. You'll need those heavy-duty pads and will likely have cramps and bleeding for a few hours after. Similar to a natural miscarriage, the bleeding lasts for one to two weeks, often with starts, stops, spotting, and clotting.

According to research, the success rate for completing a miscarriage after using misoprostol is roughly

71 to 84 percent.[5] However, some women may not experience any bleeding after they take the medication and may require another dose. If that still doesn't do anything or you only experience light bleeding, the doctor will likely have you come in for another ultrasound to see what is going on and then may advise you to do a D&C, which leads us to Option C.

Option C: Dilation and Curettage

The D&C is like a legit surgery. To be specific, it's a brief surgical procedure in which the cervix is dilated and a special instrument is used to scrape the uterine lining. You have to go in early, get prepped in the pre-op wing, and be greeted by your anesthesiologist, nurses, and your OB. I must say I was pleasantly surprised to see that my medical team, for my first miscarriage at least, did in fact resemble the cast of "Grey's Anatomy." I guess karma just had to balance out that day for me in some small way. Though we are still not even, karma! Now if they had let a basket full of puppies hang out with us while Michael and I waited, we may have been square.

After checking your vitals, you get hooked up to an IV and then just wait for an hour or so to get the surgery started. Everyone on my medical team was so kind and kept asking if I wanted a warm blanket or anything else to be comfortable, and I repeatedly refused them. Having to do a D&C was terrible and I had no desire to get comfortable, make polite chit-chat, or pretend at all that this was a pleasant experience. I felt miserable and for whatever reason needed my physical surroundings and physical experience to match my inner hell. So, in short, no blanket for me, Nurse Kristen.

---

[5] Santha, Kala Bahuleyan, et al., "Medical Management of Missed Miscarriages Using Vaginal Misoprostol—A Prospective Observational Study," Journal of Evidence-Based Medicine 4.20 (2017): 1152.

The last thing I remember before the D&C was my attractive anesthesiologist telling me that he was going to give me a "margarita to relax." I appreciated the attempt at levity, but remember, I was intent on being miserable so I just politely smiled and let the drugs take their effects. I know for some people they can remember going into the operating room and speaking to their doctor, but the last thing I remember was getting my "margarita" and then waking up in post-op with two kindly nurses by my side. I'm not sure if I woke up and started crying or if I had already been crying, but I do remember the absolute sense of despair that was waiting for me like some malevolent predator when I woke up. While I had been desperately needing this step of the process to be over, waking up and realizing that I was truly not pregnant anymore and no longer had anything growing inside of me was like hearing the news of my miscarriage all over again.

My nurse, a warm, motherly Indian woman, grabbed my hand and told me that she had experienced a miscarriage before she had her two children. She looked at me and said earnestly, "It's going to be hard, but you are going to get through this." I really needed to hear that. Eventually, I was rolled to yet another hospital room to wait for 30 minutes before I was cleared to leave the hospital. Finally. I honestly can't remember the rest of that day that well. I know I had many texts from friends wishing me well and telling me they were thinking about me. I remember comfy clothes and lying on my couch in Michael's arms with our dogs beside us and tears streaming down my face. When people asked how I was the next day, I kept saying I was relieved to have the physical part done with so I could just focus on moving forward.

But wait! The roller coaster that is miscarriage is STILL NOT DONE. I will say the physical recovery from the D&C wasn't terrible; the worst of it was that I had to wear panty liners for about a week and I wasn't able to have sex for three weeks. When we were given the "all clear," my husband and I had to use condoms for a month to prevent pregnancy as my doctor recommended that we wait at least one cycle before we try getting pregnant again.

There is nothing that makes me madder then when I'm told I can't do something. Under normal circumstances, maybe my husband I don't have sex one week because of conflicting schedules or we keep eating out at Popeyes and I just don't feel sexy when I'm bloated from delicious spicy chicken strips. But when I was told I couldn't have sex for three whole weeks, I was pissed!! All I wanted to do was go back to normal, which for me in that moment meant plunging straight into repressing everything that had happened, and having sex with my husband whenever I damn well pleased was one of the best repression techniques I could think of.

Don't worry! We followed the rules. While my resentment and unhappiness made me want to say stick it to the universe and throw the doctor's instructions straight out the window, Michael stayed strong and we slowly moved into using condoms once we hit that benchmark. Finally, some sense of normalcy, even with the annoying latex interloper...and then I started spotting every time after we had sex. I touched base with my good friend, Dr. Google, and turns out an irritated cervix after a miscarriage is fairly common. While this was my experience, there are in fact a host of unpleasant, surprising, and frustrating changes that may happen to your body following a miscarriage.

Returning to the Scene of the Crime

After you have completed whatever option you decided on (or what was decided for you), you must return to your

OB's office in a few weeks for a follow-up appointment. Let's go ahead and acknowledge the hideousness that is returning to the scene of the crime after a miscarriage. From the minute I entered the waiting room, I was reminded of my last experience there. The last time I walked through these doors, I was excitedly waiting to see my baby on the ultrasound. And when I walked out of those doors months ago, I was crying so hard that Michael had to guide me out. When we sat down, it was hard not to notice the numerous pregnant women happily waiting for their appointments. Of course, I don't know their stories. I don't know what it took for them to get to the hallowed position of actually being noticeably pregnant in an OB's waiting room. All I knew in that moment is that I wanted to get the hell out of there as quickly as possible.

My follow-up appointment after our first miscarriage was straightforward. I didn't have to undress or do another ultrasound, thank God. Instead, my doctor just asked how my bleeding was after the D&C and if I had any concerning symptoms. Fortunately, I did not have any complications and we spent the rest of our 15 minutes together discussing how long I should wait before we attempted to get pregnant again. She said I only needed to wait one cycle until I was physically ready, but that I may want to wait longer before I was emotionally ready. I went ahead and let that advice go right down the drain.

The follow-up appointment after my second miscarriage was a little more complicated. I did have to undress, and my OB did a quick pelvic exam. We had gotten testing done on the fetal tissue following my second D&C, and she discussed the results and provided us with referrals to an infertility specialist. There was that word again: infertility. It still hurt and shocked me every time I heard it. This time there were no words said about this being an "unfortunately common occurrence" and that there was nothing to suggest we wouldn't go on to have a successful pregnancy. Notably, there was no spiel about waiting a month before trying again, which was an implicit message within itself. In fact, she didn't want us to try again right away. She (and Dr. Google) thought we should get testing done before we attempted to get pregnant again. There was no straightforward path for us this time.

Mo' Money, Mo' Problems

Or in my case, *no* money because it was all gone after this next nitty-gritty aspect of the D&C. Dear readers, that shit is expensive!! Talk about adding insult to injury.

As you may recall, by the time I learned of my miscarriage, I had already had numerous medical appointments, blood draws, and ultrasounds to the point that our $3,000.00 deductible was almost tapped out. And then on top of all of that, we had to pay my doctor, the hospital where we had the D&C, and the anesthesiologist for my surgery. Maternity costs in general are ridiculous, but at least you get a baby in the end. I had to pay all of this for what? A measly anesthesia "margarita" and an empty womb. Real shitty trade if you ask me.

Not a lot of people talk about the costs of getting a D&C, but I want to share this with y'all because I think it's another part of the process that impacts you. The D&C in total with the costs of paying my OB and the hospital was approximately $4,000. When I found out how much we were going to have to pay out of pocket, I was immediately consumed with guilt and asked Michael if we should consider the medication route (Option B) even though our doctor had recommended a D&C. He gave me the reassurances that I needed, but I still couldn't shake that feeling of guilt and distress that we had to spend thousands of our hard-earned money on nothing. Twice!

The Enemy That is Time

Another nitty-gritty dose of reality to consider is the enemy that is time. I've always hated those comments about a woman's "biological clock ticking," and absolutely despise that this sentiment has become an all too real factor in my recovery. After my first miscarriage, I had the desire to immediately start trying to conceive ("TTC" in the parlance of the fertility community) again, thinking, as my OB mentioned, our first miscarriage was likely a "fluke" and our next pregnancy would be successful. Now, as we will discuss in the next chapter, it is important to give yourself some time to emotionally heal before jumping on the TTC bandwagon again. But one aspect I found particularly frustrating was having to wait till my first cycle to begin TTC again, and waiting one cycle is likely on the more liberal end of the spectrum as I know some doctors recommend waiting up to three months or more.

Why is this so challenging? Because time, just like finances, just like the course of your pregnancy, is one more thing that feels outside of your control. Once I made the decision that I was ready to have a baby, I was ready immediately, and while I knew it could take some time for us to conceive, once I saw that positive pregnancy test, a timeline had been constructed in my mind. After my first miscarriage, that timeline was wiped clean. Enter my second pregnancy and a second timeline, which was also wiped devastatingly clean. Now, instead of having a baby in June or October of 2019, I would again have to wait months after my D&C to recover, and then would need to wait for the guidance of an infertility specialist before we could TTC again, all the while being acutely aware of my biological clock continuing to tick away. Dealing with all this pain, uncertainty, and loss was so overwhelming and we were still only in the first few weeks. How would I, how could I, expect myself to keep moving forward?

Chapter 3
SURVIVING THE FIRST MONTH

This chapter is for those of you who are in the thick of it. You just found that you're having a miscarriage, and your world is rocked. Nothing makes sense. Nothing is okay. And the fact that the sun still rises, that people keep going to work, and that you are expected to continue to function like a "normal" adult feels tragic, unfair, and infuriating all at once. This is a time when "normal you" takes a backseat. You are metaphorically (maybe literally) bleeding out in the ER. Your only job this month is to survive by whatever ways necessary. Say no to demands constantly, say yes to help every time, and be as focused on yourself and your needs as much as you need to. The goal is survival, ladies.

The month of November following my first miscarriage was absolute hell for me. The day I found out about it, I passed out. No, not from shock or from anything related to my miscarriage. I passed out from a nicotine overdose. Yup. When the miscarriage was confirmed, I decided I was going to immediately jump into doing all things I had not been able to do for the last months because of pregnancy. I was going to smoke hookah (originating from India, it's used for smoking flavored tobacco), drink wine, and then take a steaming hot bath. I only made it to step one of my "I'm not pregnant anymore, so fuck everything" plan (clearly there were some flaws in my thinking).

After not smoking hookah for months and usually doing it only once a month or so with my sister after eating, I proceeded to smoke hookah for 40 minutes straight, which for you hookah newbies out there, that's quite a lot of nicotine to take in, especially if you're not a regular smoker. About 10 minutes later, Michael was trying to distract me in the kitchen with some dancing (which I usually find hilarious), but all I could focus on was how suddenly overheated I felt, how it felt like I was in a tunnel, and the next thing I remember, I woke up on the floor in his arms. I have never passed out before, but I had always imagined that when and if I ever did, it was going to be slow and graceful, reminiscent of Scarlett O'Hara, and Michael would catch me in a dip as my long hair brushed the floor. Instead, I came an inch away from banging my head onto my kitchen counter before Michael caught me, whereupon we both crashed to the floor, because apparently when I go completely limp I'm quite heavy. When I finally came to I was in a clammy sweat and walked/crawled with Michael's assistance to the welcome breeze outside, where I lay on the grass, prostrate. None of this was graceful, but it was slow. It was also messy, sad, and scary. Needless to say, I didn't get my wine or hot bath. Fucking November.

In hindsight, that story is emblematic of my time immediately following my pregnancy loss: dark but also funny. If you do get a couple of chuckles from reading it, that makes me happy, but I share it primarily to say that it's okay to be a mess, to reach occasionally for the wrong sorts of comforts because you've never walked through this. You are learning how to cope day by day, second by second.

And even if you have had a miscarriage before, the loss still feels just as painful and tragic the next time around. Indeed, while it is hard to compare the horrific experiences of two miscarriages, I found that my second carried with it an extra layer of fear and hopelessness. One miscarriage can be chalked up to simple "bad luck," not to mention that the stats of miscarriage are so high in the first trimester that many women will end up experiencing one. But two? I didn't get the speech the second time around that this was just "bad luck" or a "fluke." Instead I was told that tests would need to be run and steps would need to be taken to ensure that all was genetically normal with my husband and me. Enter in the feelings of fear and hopelessness.

No matter where you are at in your journey, if it is your first miscarriage, or your second, third, or so on, please remember there is no "good" or "right" way to respond following this loss. Much of our anxiety, in all scopes of life, is related to the idea that there is a "correct" way of doing things, and we endlessly compare what we are doing, thinking, and saying to this magical, perfect standard. As with most things in life, there is no correct answer here. There is no correct way to cope or survive in this first horrific month, but there are ways that the immediate aftermath can be more challenging that it already will be. So please give yourself permission to be messy, to be confused, to not feel like yourself, because that is all so normal.

Coming Home After a Miscarriage

One of the first actions I took after finding out about my first miscarriage was deleting my "What to expect" app on my phone. When I arrived home, I threw all the new baby flyers and folders that my OB had given me into the trash and tossed my prenatal vitamins and half-caffeine coffee into the garbage. Thankfully, my ultrasound pictures did not succumb to this insta-purge, but instead I tucked them away into a box in the back of my closet. Similar to my response after past painful breakups, I just wanted to get rid of any reminder of what had been and have my physical surroundings now reflect my emotional state – denial, essentially. I share all of this to say that you may be confronted with some painful feelings when you get home.

You may encounter reminders of your pregnancy all over your house, from the healthy snacks you stocked in your kitchen, to the ultrasound picture lying proudly on your desk, to the nursery that you may have already set up.

Based on my own experiences as well as the stories of other women who have experienced miscarriages, however, I would suggest refraining from trashing everything that reminds you of your pregnancy, and instead compile all of these items, put them in a box, and then when you feel ready, allow yourself to decide what you want to do with the contents. Maybe everything will end up in the garbage eventually, but allow yourself the time to grieve and process before taking a jackhammer to your dreams. Which leads us to…

Don't Make Any Huge Life Decisions

Getting a tattoo, converting our planned nursey room into a gym, and cutting all my hair off. These were a few ideas I contemplated in the month following my first miscarriage. I wanted to do something to memorialize our loss and our baby and convinced my husband that we should get matching tattoos. (I had an advantage here: he would've said yes to anything in the month following.) I was sure this was going to be a great experience, except I had no real idea of what I wanted to get. I came very close to copying another woman's miscarriage memorial tattoo from Pinterest. It was a beautiful tattoo, but it symbolized her story, not mine. Thankfully, those Pinterest searches soon started to fade in frequency, as did the idea and the urge to cut off all my hair. I blame movies for that one – people always cut off their hair when they're in life-changing mode.

After a traumatic event or loss, we have a desire to turn away from our pain by immersing ourselves into something new, exciting, and so all-consuming of our attention that we can no longer focus on our pain. Remember, I mentioned denial earlier? Mental health providers suggest waiting at least three months following a loss to make significant life decisions.[6] This is because, as mentioned previously, our minds, our bodies, and our thinking are all impacted following a traumatic event. This is not to say that we shouldn't ever make any changes following a loss, but research and experience have told us that it can be helpful to give ourselves a little bit of time to process and grieve before we begin making irrevocable changes.

I will say that of the ideas I had, I only ended up following through on one of them immediately.

We converted the planned nursery into a gym. We ripped up all the carpet and over the course of a week filled it with workout equipment. It was a great distraction, and I still use the room all the time. And yet, I feel a stab of sadness as I recall how excited I was to change that room into a nursey, and as I remember the times I went in there and daydreamed about how the crib would look perfect against the back wall, giving the baby a view of the tall, beautiful trees outside the window.

Of course, it's not impossible to convert a room back, but right now it feels like a lot. And now, months later, I wish that my husband and I had waited a little longer before making this decision and taking this step because it almost feels as if we were trying to erase part of our dreams because they were too painful to hold on to. Maybe it's what we needed at the time, because I'm not sure what it would be like to walk past that painfully empty

---

6   Dansky, B. S., Roth, S., & Kronenberger, W. G., "The Trauma Constellation Identification Scale: A Measure of he Psychological Impact of a Stressful Life Event," Journal of Traumatic Stress, no. 3 (1990): 557–572.

room and be reminded of those dreams and hopes we had. Like I said earlier, there are no "right" or "correct" decisions here, but as a general rule of thumb, give yourself time and space to grieve. If there are changes or things you want to do in your life, by all means start planning them and dreaming about them but see if you can give yourself even one month before taking action.

Going Back to Work

My job as a psychologist was both a blessing and a curse. On one hand, I sincerely welcomed the distraction of immersing myself in someone else's life, experiences, feelings, and thoughts. The further from anything baby related the better. Oh, you want to talk about your codependent tendencies? Awesome. Your partner who may have narcissistic traits? I'm all about it!

The not so great part was that along with wanting distance from all things babies, there was definitely a part of me that wanted distance from all things pain. A fairly large component of being a therapist is being a witness to so much pain, despair, anguish, and grief, and while I am usually all about that, it was so much harder for me to hold these painful feelings without letting some of my own feelings get intermixed, which then led to the shame gremlins in my head saying, "You're a shitty therapist thinking about yourself when you should be focused on your client." Shame gremlins get me every time. Enter my survival guide for the first month: Work edition.

First, I cancelled. A LOT. When I didn't feel like I could show up for my clients in the way that they deserved, I cancelled. Now, I'm so grateful and fortunate that I had that option, but at a certain point, that option ran out because I needed to be there for my clients. And I know for some of you out there, it was never an option from the beginning. You had to show up because your job was on the line, your family's financial security depended on you, or there were logistical matters that made cancelling a non-starter.

This leads to my next survival lesson. Share what you need and ask for support. I am a prototypical peacemaker (Enneagram type 9 for any of my enneagram lovers out there), meaning I am agreeable and accommodating, and always aim to make sure everyone else is happy and has what they need. But that month, it was all about me.

If you are at work and have shared your story with even one person, enlist that person for support. Tell them you need extra help on a project or that no, you cannot take on anything new this month. If you haven't or don't feel comfortable sharing the details of your loss, keep it vague, but still communicate what you need. We often have the idea that if we say no, chaos will ensue and things will fall apart. But this is usually not the case. Even those in the Oval Office have people who can pick up the slack if they are absent. Your work will survive without you there.

We also often have the idea that if we say no to something or say what we need, people will be disappointed in us, confused, shocked, upset, or any other myriad of negative emotions. I want you to picture someone at work you care about—hell, even someone you don't care too much about—and imagine them in your situation, with your thoughts and feelings. Now imagine them asking for some extra support or grace. What did that feel like? Were you disappointed, angry, or upset with them? Or, did you feel compassion or concern? Again, I recognize that this may not be a universal reaction, but in the majority of cases, your coworkers, just like you, will respond with empathy and concern.

Third, give yourself so much grace. For most of us, we have an expectation for how we show up and perform at work. For this first month, at least, go ahead and chuck those expectations out the window. For example, at my work meetings, I often like to show up as my cheerful, happy self. In the first month following my loss, I was quiet and often unsmiling and I just let myself be. Usually I'd berate myself if I didn't speak up in a meeting or volunteer for an opportunity, but this month I let my standards shift. All I needed to do was be present for my clients and survive. That is it.

It brings to mind my first experience of hot yoga. For those of you who haven't experienced the joys of hot yoga, imagine yourself in a 100+ degrees Fahrenheit room sweating it out while doing challenging body poses. The minute you enter that room, the air leaves your lungs. You know it's going to be hot, but you can't prepare for the way that the heat feels like punch to your gut, making it hard to breathe or even think for the first few minutes. The instructor, picking up on my clear newness to the class and obvious panic, told me that my only job today was to stay in the room. Even if I did not attempt any of the poses and remained lying down the whole time, that was good enough. I just needed to survive the heat.

For the first month following your loss, you just need to stay in the room and survive the heat. Don't expect yourself to be like everyone else, who seem to be completing the poses effortlessly while are you struggling to get air into your lungs. Even if it feels like all you are doing is just lying there not doing anything at all, you are. By waking up, by surviving, you are doing everything you need to.

Find Outlets for Pain

One of the first questions I ask all my new clients is how do you take care of yourself when you are feeling stressed? I ask this because it is so important that we all have intentional ways of taking care of ourselves because, damn, life can get tough. And that is certainly the case following a miscarriage. It is vital to ensure that you give yourself time to grieve your loss and that you identify specific, tailored methods to help you process your feelings and pain following a miscarriage.

For myself, I often sought out support from family and friends, began journaling regularly, and went to therapy on a weekly basis. As I've mentioned, I'm somewhat of a biased source when it comes to therapy, but I will say in my own experience, I found engaging in individual and couples therapy as well as a miscarriage support group to be all so helpful in processing and unpacking my emotions and reactions to my losses. If going to therapy or a support group is not an option due to time or financial constraints, I would strongly recommend getting connected with an online support community of women who have experienced miscarriage(s). The support of your family and friends is invaluable, but the support from those who have walked this same journey is so meaningful.

Now, let's get real here. I understand that sometimes life gets so busy that it can be challenging for us to even find time to set aside for our grief. If you fall into that category, here are some suggestions for you. Use your commute home (not on the way to work unless you want to be a crying mess when you arrive or you have a superhuman ability to compartmentalize your emotions) or even your time in the shower to let yourself cry or process how you are feeling. I found a great podcast on miscarriages and an audiobook on grief[7] that I listened to every day on the ride home from work, and used that time as an opportunity to reflect on my inner experience. And on the days I had a passenger and was not in the right headspace to listen to my podcast or book, I just allowed myself to cry and grieve in the shower.

An important caveat here is to find the balance between making space for your grief and not forcing yourself to think about your miscarriage if you are not in the headspace to do it. While I listened to my podcast or audiobook almost every day on my way home for that first month, there were some days I needed a break from my grief, and I would listen to sappy music and zone out. Figure out what you need and be flexible with it.

Exercise: What Do I Need?

Create three columns on a piece of paper and label column one as "People," column two as "Places," and column three as "Things." Under each column identify and write down what people, places, and things have provided you with care in the past. Use this list as a survival guide template to get you through your first month. For example, after identifying the people, places, and things that have provided you support in the past, consider how you can incorporate these elements into your life on a regular basis. I have shared my survival guide below.

---

[7] They were, respectively, "The Life After Miscarriage Podcast by Shelly Mettling"; Megan Devine's It's OK That You're Not OK: Meeting Grief and Loss in a Culture That Doesn't Understand (Sounds True Publishing 2017).

People	Places	Things
Michael, Sheila, Tiffany, Cherlyn, Mere, and Alex.	Living room couch, backyard deck, tennis courts, yoga studio, parents' house, and dog park.	Journaling, reading, listening to podcasts, self-compassion exercises, therapy, exercising, crying, volunteering, date nights with my husband, and playing with my dogs.

Chapter 4

HOW TO GET THE SUPPORT YOU NEED

I could only hold in the news of my first pregnancy for two days. Two measly days. For someone whose livelihood depends on maintaining confidentiality, you would think I'd have better restraint. For all past, current, and future clients, as well as psychology ethics board members, I always keep my clients' confidentiality. I promise! But when it comes to sharing exciting news about myself, I cannot hold it in for more than an hour, so I actually deserve some kudos for making it two whole days (cue the applause).

We found out on a Thursday that I was pregnant, and by that Monday, Michael, my family, his family, and my boss all knew about it. There was a brief moment where Michael and I questioned whether it was a good idea to tell so many people before we reached the "safe" 12-week mark, but I righteously and passionately told Michael and anyone who would listen that I didn't think we should keep such good news silent. If the worst did happen and we did have a miscarriage, well, we should talk about it! This news does not deserve to be stigmatized or relegated to the shadows. Well, self-righteous me, meet current me, writing a book all about miscarriage. No regrets, right?

You may wonder, why devote an entire chapter to getting support after your miscarriage? It seems fairly obvious. If you are struggling or need help, ask your friends and family. But, as you may have gathered thus far, nothing is simple when it comes to life after miscarriage. For example, if you made the decision to tell people about your pregnancy early on, you will also then face the task of telling people you have had a miscarriage. Now there is upside and downside to this. The upside is that you don't have to play pretend with people, acting as if everything is okay when your entire world has fallen apart. Additionally, I do feel like there is some sense of relief in sharing and telling your story. Often, after we have experienced a tragedy or trauma, people assume we wouldn't want to talk about it because why would we want to relive it? But let me tell you, the news about my miscarriage was playing on repeat in my head, and the few times it felt less overwhelming was when I shared it with someone safe.

Author, psychologist, and grief researcher Megan Devine writes that, in grief, "We share our stories to make sense of what has happened."[8] Our sense of past and future is fundamentally disrupted by a miscarriage. While I thought I was having a healthy pregnancy, I found out I wasn't, and while I thought I was planning a future with my husband and our baby, I wasn't. My mind didn't know how to make sense of this once beautiful portrait that felt like it had been ripped apart and shredded. So, I needed to tell that story again, and again, and again until I could make some sense of it and integrate it into my narrative.

The downside is that once you tell people, it's hard to hold it together when your loved ones are looking at you with "I'm so worried" and "I'm so sorry" eyes. Very compassionate looks for sure, but hard when you are expected to keep functioning as a normal adult. Sometimes it can be a nice distraction to play pretend and take a break from the devastation that is your world after a miscarriage. Ultimately, I imagine most of us have a mix of people we feel safe with and can share with, while there are some people in our lives we will intentionally decide to

---

[8] Devine, Megan, It's OK that You're Not OK: Meeting Grief and Loss in a Culture that Doesn't Understand (Louisville: Sounds True Publishing 2017).

keep on the fringes, for now at least.

Okay, so you have decided to tell some people about your miscarriage. Maybe your sister, maybe your mother-in-law, maybe your boss. Now prepare yourself for some lovingly given BS.

I want to make the disclaimer that there is no "right" thing to say after a miscarriage, but there are definitely statements you can make that veer towards being helpful and validating while there are other statements that are dismissive and completely unhelpful. Here are a few examples of those; a little later, I'll give you examples of the helpful things people said.

- All the unhelpful things people told me:
- God has a plan for you. (GAG.)
- Don't worry. Everything is going to be okay. (How in the world would you know that?)
- Your time will come soon. (Could I borrow that crystal ball when you're done with it?)
- There wasn't really a baby yet, right? (Tell that to my sore boobs, nausea, weight gain, and cherished hopes.)
- Well the silver lining is that it happened so early. (Silver lining for me or for you?)
- You weren't attached yet because it happened so early, right? (Is this a question or a demand?)

Again, I know all these statements were given with the best of intentions, but let's be real. They were also given with the intention to decrease and distance me from my own pain—though it is perfectly acceptable and even necessary to sit in (i.e. not deny) our own pain, for a time at least. Additionally, these statements gave the speakers a way to distance themselves from my pain, because they didn't know what to do with it or how to fix it. As a society, particularly Western societies, we struggle to allow ourselves and others to sit in pain. We want to be happy

NOW, we want to stop being sad NOW. Yet, as I tell so many of my clients, we have a spectrum of emotions because we are supposed to allow ourselves to experience them. In other words, if I feel sad one day, I don't immediately need to play "detective" to figure out why I'm sad and how to fix it; I can just accept that this is a normal part of the human experience and let it be. Grief is unfortunately a universal aspect of the human experience and not something that can or should be washed away by well wishes or clichéd sayings.

Fuck Silver Linings... At Least the Ones Other People Tell Yc

As a therapist, I have heard so many clients describe how invalidated, dismissed, unheard, and unseen they feel when someone tells them to "look at the silver lining." While silver linings may inspire hope in some, they often send the message that it's not okay for you to focus on the hurt you are feeling and that instead you need to turn that frown upside down by focusing on the "positives." If you have decided to take the path of sharing your miscarriage with others, be prepared to hear some silver-lining statements and/or "at least" statements, similar to those I have listed above. Again, you don't need my permission, but please know it is okay to say fuck the silver linings – either out loud, to yourself, or to your loved ones (maybe not in those specific words, but whatever works). It's okay to sit in your pain and to feel loss, despair, anger, and grief. As I mentioned in the beginning of this book, this is a big deal and there is no need to tie up your grief with a pretty bow and say everything is going to be okay. Maybe there will come a time when you feel ready to move forward however that looks for you, but until then, let's call a spade a spade. Miscarriage fucking sucks. Period.

Explaining Empathy

After saying fuck the silver linings (again either internally or externally, and perhaps in nicer language depending on your mood), it can be so helpful to share with your loved ones the support you need from them. Notice I stated "loved ones" here specifically. When it comes to your acquaintances, distant friends, and certain coworkers, you may not want to extend the energy it takes to describe what you need and it may not be worth it to take that step if this is not a person you plan to seek support from in the future. However, when it comes to your loved ones, those people whose support you really depend on, it's important to let them know what you need and how you need it.

Empathy is not something that should be taught, right? Wrong! Empathy is defined as "the action of understanding, being aware of, being sensitive to, and vicariously experiencing the feelings, thoughts, and experience of another of either the past or present without having the feelings, thoughts, and experience fully communicated in an objectively explicit manner."[9] Said another way, psychologist, researcher, and prolific author Brené Brown writes, "Empathy is communicating that incredibly healing message of you are not alone."[10] It is a skill that takes practice. Providing empathy to another person is hard work because it means that you are exposed to their pain and you are sitting with them in it, which can be so powerful. I hope you have had the experience of your loved ones providing you with much deserved empathy, and it's important to recognize it when it occurs because that's the support we need to keep going.

---

[9] https://www.merriam-webster.com/dictionary/empathy
[10] Brown, Brené, The Power of Vulnerability: Teachings of Authenticity, Connection, and Courage (Louisville: Sounds True Publishing: 2013).

For example, I was venting once to a good friend about how annoyed and hurt I was about some of the statements people had made when I shared about miscarriage. She sat with me in my pain and validated that those reactions were not okay and that it sucked to hear those things. She also asked me if there were any statements that were helpful to hear. Damn, good question. It took some digging, but here are a few great examples of empathy.

- All the helpful things people told me:
- This could happen again and if it does, we will get through it. (That was a gem from the hubs.)
- You are allowed to feel whatever you want whenever you want.
- You don't need my permission, but if you need to, you can say no. You can take another day. (From my awesome boss.)
- Even if we don't ask, always know you can talk about it.
- I still feel upset about my miscarriage a year after it happened. (Some people may experience this as distressing, but I found it SO validating. You mean I'm not crazy for feeling this way?)
- Your ghost baby is probably in the walls. (This was Michael's 4-year-old nephew's reaction to my miscarriage. I found this helpful because here was this child talking about the elephant in the room most people were avoiding. And also because it was a morbidly hilarious statement and it felt comforting to think my "ghost baby" was still with me. Thanks, Jack. You're one of the good ones.)

Asking for Empathy

Okay, now we know what empathy means and what it looks like, but how do we ask for it? It can be so challenging to ask our loved ones for the support we need. First, we are already struggling with an avalanche of

53

painful emotions, so taking the energy to explain to someone what we need when we are barely making it through the day is exhausting. Believe me, I know. Second, I found myself feeling cruel in telling my loved ones that their uplifting statements of hope were actually not helpful and I needed something different from them. I will acknowledge that, for my first miscarriage, I completely chickened out and instead of telling my loved ones what I needed, I kept my "Fuck your silver linings" in my head and ranted about those thoughts to Michael later. Not a very helpful approach.

For my second miscarriage, I was all out of fucks to give, and when my mother compassionately and kindly told me everything was going to be okay, I turned to her said, "I know you mean well, but we don't know that. So, please just let me be sad and be sad with me." She seemed taken aback and hurt and didn't know what to say, so she just sat with me silently for a while. I eventually went and hid in the bathroom because that silence felt so uncomfortable. I felt guilty and uncomfortable with rocking the proverbial boat of my family's dynamics, but mostly I felt relieved I didn't have to pretend that I agreed that everything was going to be okay. Later, when my sister optimistically offered, "At least you guys will be able to get testing done this time," I turned to her and said, "I know you are trying to help, but I'm not trying to look at the positive right now. Can we just talk about how much this sucks instead?" She was momentarily taken aback and said nothing.

These were not transformative moments where I shared with my family what I needed and they immediately were able to provide that for me. Instead, it felt awkward and painful for all parties involved, but it was worth it because just a few weeks later, my mother and I had one of the most honest conversations we ever had. I took the risk of sharing with her that Michael and I had started considering the very real possibility that we may never be able to conceive, and we had now wondered what our life would look like without children. Instead of saying everything was going to be okay, my mother acknowledged that this was a potential possibility for us and shared that she sometimes wondered what her life would be like if she had not had children. She continually reassured me that she was so grateful to have had me and my siblings (I have no doubt about this; my mom has made it clear that my siblings and I are her world) but allowed there to be space for us to discuss how a life could be meaningful without kids. Hearing that from my mother, who I had previously worried would be disappointed if I didn't have kids, was so powerful and freeing. And my sister, my logical, aggressively optimistic sister, eventually started asking me open-ended questions like "What was that like for you?" and saying validating statements that were as simple as "I'm sorry this is happening. It's not okay."

When asking for support, while it's important to share what you don't need, it's even more important to share what you do need. Telling someone, "Hey, it's not helpful when you say this" is a good place to start and takes a lot of courage, but they need to know what you do need instead. It's also so important, if you can find the energy in you, to share your appreciation with them when you do receive the support you are asking for. With both my mother and sister, I told them that I so appreciated them offering me empathy instead of silver linings, and space instead of solutions. My hope is that from this experience, my family will begin to learn a new language of love and support towards each other.

Finding My Own Silver Linings

A couple of months after our first miscarriage, I was having a conversation with Michael—well, more a rant-fest, with him listening and shaking his head at the appropriate places as I railed about the insensitivity and dismissiveness of silver linings. "How can there be anything good at all about a miscarriage?" I said. "Why do people feel so uncomfortable with pain that they need to put a positive spin on a tragedy? I fucking hate silver linings!!"

After a while of listening, my husband asked, "Are all silver linings bad?" I stared at him. Had he not just heard my rant?! I was about to get amped up again when I paused and considered the question further. Did I really hate the idea of searching for meaning in suffering? I mean what kind of masochistic weirdo would I be if I never wanted to find the glimmer of hope in something? One of my favorite books, Man's Search for Meaning by Victor Frankl, is all about searching for meaning in the darkest of places. Frankl, a psychiatrist who wrote the premises for his book on scraps of paper while he was imprisoned in a Nazi concentration camp writes: "Suffering ceases to be suffering at the moment it finds meaning."[11] And upon reflection, I realized amidst all our pain, my husband and I had found deepened meaning, such as forming deeper relationships with friends I discovered had also experienced miscarriages.

What I took from this conversation is not that I needed to find the positive in my miscarriage, but that I could CHOOSE to find meaning in my suffering. Loss has a way of illuminating and potentially shifting some of our priorities. For me, that meant leaning into my values of connection and learning. I connected with friends that I had known for years on a deeper and more vulnerable level than ever before. I can choose to feel grateful for the friendships that

---

[11] Frankl, V. E., Man's Search for Meaning: An Introduction to Logotherapy (New York: Simon & Schuster 1984).

I have leaned into, I can choose to appreciate the courage it took for me to acknowledge my suffering, and I can choose to write a book on how this experience has profoundly changed me, with the hopes of helping other women who have experienced a miscarriage.

The important caveat to me here is that I was the one to label what felt hopeful and meaningful to me amidst all this pain. This is important to emphasize because no one else can tell you how to make meaning out of your loss. No one can tell you how this experience has changed you, and no can define for you the hope, meaning, and depth that you may or may not get out of experiencing a miscarriage. And believe me it took weeks for me to get to that place where I was able to acknowledge the gift in being able to reach a deeper level of knowing with some of my friends and with myself. If you never get to that place, that is completely okay. This is your process and yours alone to define.

The Community

Whether you asked for it or not, you have joined a community of women who instantly know what you have been through and who are walking the same terrain you are. Welcome to the not-so-secret society of women who have experienced a miscarriage. I had a couple of friends and clients over the years who had a miscarriage, but as Michael and I continued to share our story with others, I was shocked by how many women had experienced one or multiple miscarriages. The stats tell you one in three women will experience a miscarriage,[12] but damn it's like

---

[12] Cohain, Judy Slome, Rina E. Buxbaum, and David Mankuta, "Spontaneous First Trimester Miscarriage Rates Per Woman Among Parous Women with 1 or More Pregnancies of 24 Weeks or More," *BMC Pregnancy and Childbirth* no. 17.1 (2017): 437.

everyone we knew, especially those who had children, had experienced at least one. It got to the point that when Michael would tell me that he had told someone about our experience, my follow-up question would be – did they have one too? And I swear, nine times out of ten, they did!!

Obviously, this isn't great news, as my enthusiasm may imply. But there is such a strong feeling of connection and a sense of being known that you experience when speaking to someone who has gone through the same thing. For example, I found out about our first miscarriage on a Wednesday and was back at work the next day. A coworker kindly and unknowingly asked how pregnancy was going and I immediately broke down crying. She scooted closer to me and said, "I'm so sorry. I know nothing I can say will make this better, but I'm here with you." And I continued to cry as three more of my coworkers walked in, listened to my story, and all gathered around me. Several of the women present had personal experienced with miscarriage. Our age, backgrounds, and specific experiences were all different, but there was an instant feeling of "You get this." They listened to me, they shared their stories, and one of the women, at my request, told me step by step what to expect from the D&C procedure.

After a tragedy, we often don't know what to say. I know I've attempted to comfort people in the past and have said the wrong thing and have felt awkward as hell. And while there is definitely no "right" thing to say after a miscarriage, talking to people who have been through it, who have experienced the raw pain, the physical torture, the chaotic waves of grief, is SO validating. What I most needed to hear was that it was okay that I was feeling devastated. For whatever reason, I had this question in my head: "Am I making this bigger than it really is? Is my reaction too much?" because I truly was shocked by the depth of despair particularly in the few days after hearing the news. My coworkers who had experienced miscarriages told me about how they too still feel their grief months or even years later. While for some that may have been disheartening to hear, for me it was almost as if I had been given permission. I had permission to grieve, to allow this to feel as gigantic as it did, and to mourn however I needed to.

You don't need my or anyone's permission to grieve, but just in case, like me, you've experienced a moment of doubt, a question of whether your reaction is justified, let me say now, you have permission to mourn, to feel devastated, to be not okay for a really long time, maybe to never be okay in the way you once were. You have permission to fall apart and to need others to help put you back together. You have permission to cry everywhere and anywhere. I know I did. And you have permission to make this a big deal because it is. It so is! I would encourage you, if possible, to seek out support through women who have been through this, whether that it is through friends, a support group, or an online community. Believe me, it makes a world of difference.

Exercise: Fuck the Silver Linings

- Write a list of the most unhelpful things people told you. Every single one that comes to mind. If you are feeling up to it or are feeling particularly sassy, write your response to each of them as I did above. Your response can be as simple as "No!" or it can be a description of what that statement made you feel, such as "Hearing this makes me feel sad and dismissed." Expletives in the response section are not required, but highly encouraged. Now, destroy that list. Rip it up, burn it, throw it in a shredder. Get rid of it because those words are not your truth.

- Write a list of all the helpful things people told you. Put that list somewhere close so that on the days you need comfort, you have those compassionate, empathetic words handy. If you feel up to it, reach out to those folks whose words make up that list and share your appreciation. I promise it feels good. Both of my lists are above for reference.

Chapter 5

THE RELATIONSHIP AFTER MISCARRIAGE

Our Story

People often assume that if you are a couples' therapist, you must have the healthiest and most mature relationship. And that assumption is spot-on. Just kidding. While I do think Michael and I have a generally healthy and loving relationship, we have difficulties just like any other couple. A miscarriage, however, does not fall in the realm of "difficulties." No, a miscarriage is a trauma, and trauma can rock even the strongest and "healthiest" of couples. It certainly rocked our relationship.

When we found out the news of the first miscarriage, I remember turning to Michael, seeing his shocked face, and immediately feeling the slow roll of tears down my face. He held me and said we were going to be okay. All I could focus on in that moment was the devastation I was experiencing and I said, "I can't believe this is happening." Michael then said several statements that have been seared into my brain, statements he would later apologize for, including: "At least it happened early," "You weren't that attached to it, right?" and "The silver lining is that there wasn't a baby anyway." Each of these statements felt like a hammer to my already shattered heart, but my shock was so heavy that while I heard and registered these comments, I purposefully shifted my attention from them because I knew doing so would cause me to lash out at him which I knew I didn't want to do.

Why wouldn't I want to lash out at him? I think we can

agree that what he was saying was pretty insensitive, but even in the pit of despair, there was part of me that knew while I was having my own reactions to loss, so was my husband. He was processing this trauma in the only way he knew how, which meant automatically reassuring me and himself through forced optimism and avoidance. Michael* experienced a challenging childhood rife with his own traumas (I won't explain any further because that's his story to tell), and some tiny part of me could recognize that he had learned to cope this way as a result of numerous painful experiences. So, I didn't say anything. I didn't say that his words felt so invalidating and dismissive that I felt completely alone. I didn't say that I felt insurmountably far from him in that moment. Instead, I called my parents, my siblings, and my friends, and we went home.

When we got there, Michael held me and asked if he should still go on the trip he was supposed to leave for later that same day. Michael does woodworking as a hobby and side business and had a woodworking conference in Austin that same day. While every fiber in my being wanted him to remain by my side, I told him it was fine if he went – that there was nothing that needed to be done now anyway. There was no point in him missing this trip. He asked me repeatedly if it was okay, and I clearly said yes every time without acknowledging the resounding no my heart was saying. And then he left. He called me an hour after he had driven away, perhaps sensing without my words that it was mistake for him to have left so soon after we had experienced the first real trauma in our relationship. He said he regretted leaving and that he could come home if I needed him. I again repeated, I was fine. There was nothing he could do here, which was true.

And that was true, technically. There was nothing to be done—but everything to be said, felt, and experienced.

All of which I determined I was going to have to do on my own.

The rest of that day and the next were the worst days of my life to date. I cried constantly and even when surrounded by my loving and compassionate family and friends, I felt so crushingly alone because the one person who was really in this with me, whose loss mirrored my own, was not there. A part of me also questioned the validity of my devastation. If Michael could leave, if he could go to a conference and carry on like everything was normal the same day we heard the news that we were no longing having a baby, why was I falling apart? What was wrong with me that I was so broken while he seemed so completely whole?

At some point the next day Michael sent me a picture of him smiling widely with other woodworkers around him. At the exact moment he sent that picture, I had been staring at the bathroom mirror, willing myself to stop crying so I could finish applying my makeup and get ready for work. Seeing his happiness while I was not even able to stem my tears for a moment created a gulf for me. I had always felt so close and connected to Michael our entire relationship. He was my person. But in that moment, I had never felt so distant from him. It was as if he was living a completely different reality than me.

But I didn't share that or acknowledge that gulf to him. Instead I texted back: "Cute! So glad you are having a good time." There was no sarcasm there. I really was glad he was okay. Yet, at the same time, his being okay just made me feel more alone in my devastation. Somehow I was able to stop crying long enough to put my makeup on, and I went to work and made it through my few appointments, crying on the way to work and back and during my meeting with my coworkers, but I made it. When I got home, Michael was there waiting, home days earlier than he was expected to be. He hugged me and apologized again and again for leaving. He said he didn't know what he had been thinking, but that a part of him knew all along that he made the wrong decision and that he just didn't know what to do.

He held me while I cried and I shared with him the devastation I had felt, the isolation, and how his words and actions had affected me. I also acknowledged that I wished I could have found it in me to tell him what I needed instead of pretending that I was okay when I was anything but. He was worried that I was upset with him, and truly I wasn't. Neither of us had a playbook of what this was supposed to look like, how we were supposed to respond individually and to each other in the face of this loss. The only thing I knew is that I needed, we needed, to figure it out together. We lay on our couch for hours talking, crying, and holding each other as the wide gulf between us disappeared.

Mourning Together, but Differently

Any kind of loss or trauma impacts us differently based on our backgrounds, personalities, cultures, and unique ways of viewing the world. Additionally, while both partners in a miscarriage certainly can experience a sense of loss, their experiences may vary widely.[13] Objectively, the partner whose body miscarried is the one who experiences the physical symptoms of pregnancy and miscarriage and, subsequently, is the one who must deal with the physical toll that a miscarriage or surgery has on her body. For

---

[13] Hutti, M. H., Armstrong, D. S., Myers, J. A., & Hall, L. A., "Grief Intensity, Psychological Well-Being, and the Intimate Partner Relationship in the Subsequent Pregnancy After a Perinatal Loss," *Journal of Obstetric, Gynecologic, and Neonatal Nursing*, no. 44(1), (2015): 42–50.

many women, growing the baby inside of them certainly increases the bond and connection they have with their pregnancy. Their partners do not have access to this particular aspect of a miscarriage and thus may need some guidance in understanding what their partner is going through.

Additionally, while both partners will have their own emotional reactions to this loss, this again may differ—and differ wildly. One partner may feel furious and betrayed by her body or the world, while another may just feel devastatingly numb. One may want to share their feelings with any passing stranger, while another may become withdrawn, reticent. Partners may also have different interpretations of the magnitude of the loss. For many women, they become a mother the minute that pregnancy test says positive. They make lifestyle changes, giving up things they enjoy for the good of their child, from alcohol to rock climbing. And they already start experiencing some of the familiar tides of parenthood such as fatigue and an intense desire to protect this little one growing inside of them. While some partners may also instantly feel that connection to their child, for many who are not carrying the child, they become a parent the minute they meet their baby in the delivery room.

How to Support your Partner

With such drastically different experiences, how can partners support each other in a miscarriage? With care, of course – both care and the acronym C.A.R.E.

Curiosity: Approach your partner with curiosity. Seek to understand what their experience is like without making assumptions such as "He won't get it because he didn't carry the baby." I often will ask my couples in therapy, "Do you want to be married or do you want to be right?" This can be amended to "Do you want to be in this relationship, or do you want to be right?" If the answer is the former, then use compassionate curiosity to understand what your partner is feeling. While my husband and I certainly had different reactions to the miscarriage, through discussions imbued with curiosity I was surprised to hear how much being a father meant to him and how much he mourned not having that chance, at least for now. I have some helpful questions to guide this discussion in the exercise at the end of this chapter.

Acknowledge: Your process is just that – yours. Acknowledge and respect that your partner may be at a different place than you or have different needs than you. For example, I am the type that needs to talk about what I am feeling ALL THE TIME. I clearly found the right calling. My husband, on the other hand, certainly wanted to offer me all the space I needed to process what I was feeling, but what he needed at times was having some distance and distraction from our loss. And when that occurred, he would gently share with me that he was there with me and wanted to talk about this, but that he needed some time to process his own feelings on a run and would be happy to continue this conversation later. I appreciated his sharing what he needed, and it gave me the gentle nudge I needed to engage in some self-soothing exercises such as journaling.

Rituals: After a trauma, a couple can experience disconnection and isolation within their relationship. It is important to be mindful of this and to create opportunities for closeness and support. Rituals are a great way of increasing connection in a relationship. For example, if couples wanted to develop a ritual around the miscarriage, it could be journaling together every Sunday or reading a chapter of a book on miscarriage together every other night. Other rituals for connection include doing morning yoga together or having dinner together every night. Essentially, a ritual of connection is a consistent habit or activity you engage in with your partner designed to increase closeness and connection.

E: Explore and explain: As mentioned numerous times now, your and your partner's experience of the miscarriage may vary widely, and even if it doesn't, it is so important for you to take the time to explore and explain to your partner what you are feeling and what you need. As evidenced from my story, you can get into some real hot water by keeping your thoughts and feelings hidden from your partner. It's hard and confusing to make sense of what is going on in your mind after this loss, but even saying that is enough to help your partner know where you are at. And hopefully, using some of the questions listed at the end of this chapter will help clarify what you are feeling and needing.

Being Physically Present

Another way of supporting each other concerns all those lovely doctor's appointments. As mentioned previously, the partner who is physically experiencing the miscarriage will have her own unique challenges, and that includes the multiple doctor's appointments before and after a miscarriage diagnosis is made. One of the most helpful and supportive actions my Michael took was coming with me to each and every appointment. This meant the exciting appointments in the beginning when we got to see our baby growing, the tedious and anxiety-filled blood-draw appointments when we were at the point of needing to confirm by my hCG level that I was indeed having a miscarriage, all the way to being there during both of my D&C surgeries and my follow-up appointments weeks after the surgeries.

I can't emphasize enough what a difference it makes to have your partner physically present during these appointments. After a miscarriage, or even in early pregnancy when you are feeling anxious, going to the OB can be an emotionally exhausting experience. I initially felt excitement, then anxiety, then fear, then loss, then anger, and then just some mixture of all of the above. Having Michael there meant the world to me, and I so needed both his physical and emotional support during those latter appointments because I was often so upset that I could barely answer the doctor's or nurse's questions.

Pro tip: I would recommend having a certain phone game or other mindless distracting activity available to make that waiting room more tolerable. This was another way Michael showed up for me—coming prepared with several games on his phone to engage me while we waited. Being able to have fun with him in a place that was imbued with so much pain was so needed, and as an added bonus, I've gotten really great at virtual flip cup.

Let's Talk About Sex

Let's talk about sex after a miscarriage. As I mentioned earlier, your sex life may be on a brief hiatus depending on what treatment is needed. After both D&C's, I was told I needed to abstain from sex (or inserting tampons) for three weeks and then after that it was off to the races. Right? Well...that's where it gets a little more complicated. While after a few weeks my body was healed, my emotional healing was a little less linear. I remember wanting to jump right back into our normal sex life once we were given the green light, in a desire to get back to some sense of normalcy. But we had to use a condom and that was not normal for us. It was hard not to be reminded of the miscarriage the moment I saw that condom, and I will say that on more than one occasion it was a real mood killer for me. Apart from being a herald of our loss, the condom also meant we weren't getting pregnant any time soon. Damn, those were some symbolic condoms.

I wish I could say that some epiphany hit me and I was able to cope with the changes in our sex life and find the silver lining, but remember I say fuck silver linings. The truth was that after both miscarriages, our sex life changed. We were first devastated, then grieving, and then still processing. What helped us during this uncertain time was being completely transparent with each other. What that meant in this context was I told my husband if I didn't feel quite ready to have sex yet, and I told him when my cervix was irritated after sex a few weeks after my D&C. How's that for pillow talk? While these conversations weren't necessarily fun, they were SO necessary. My husband knows me well enough to know when I'm feeling it and when I'm really not, and on top of everything else I was dealing with, I didn't have the energy to pretend like everything automatically went back to baseline.

This transparency worked both ways. I encouraged and so appreciated when Michael shared with me his experience of how our intimacy changed for him after our miscarriages. I remember one particularly raw discussion on a car ride home after dinner when Michael shared that he noticed himself approaching intimacy with me with a new lens of caution and reserve. He wanted to be respectful of where I was at physically and emotionally, and he also grieved the easy and powerful connection we previously had in our sex life. He expressed feeling helpless and confused, which had made him hesitant to initiate physical contact. I wanted to automatically reassure him and tell him nothing had changed and he didn't have to approach me any differently. But that just wasn't true. I was changed. He was changed. Our intimacy was changed. And we needed to talk about it.

Not to mention, your body goes through so much after a miscarriage. You are pregnant for weeks, maybe months, which creates a hormonal roller coaster and a plethora of new physical symptoms that can all affect the comfort you feel in your body and your desire for intimacy. Additionally, during pregnancy, your relationship with your body changes. You often become protective and aware in a way that you were not before. You may marvel at the miracle that your body is growing this little human inside of you. After a miscarriage, the hormonal roller coaster continues, a variety of physical symptoms may persist, and instead of marveling over your body, you may start to feel disappointment, resentment, and disconnection towards it. This will be further explored in Chapter 7. All of these changes may, understandably, have an impact on your desire to have sex.

I am a huge advocate for discussing your sexuality and your intimacy needs with your partner. So do yourself and your partner a favor and be open with where you are at. Share about your physical and emotional healing. Give yourself grace and know that it is normal to have decreased libido after a miscarriage. The hormonal changes alone are enough to impact our sex drives, not to mention that grief certainly takes a heavy toll on our desire to knock boots. It took us a couple of months, but through (sometimes painful) honesty and vulnerability, we got our groove back and then some.

Couples Therapy

Of course the couples therapist recommends couples therapy, but, as with most of this book, I speak from personal experience – from both sides of the couch. I had been futilely trying to convince Michael to go to couples therapy for years prior to our miscarriage. Not because we had any huge issues I was concerned about, but because I always think it is such a great, proactive decision for couples to seek help and find a space to intentionally explore their relationship even if there are no huge grenades going off. It's *after* the grenades have gone off and we are all standing in the carnage that most couples come to therapy, which can prove difficult for all parties concerned. Another important aspect of couples therapy is that there is so much valuable information on the internet and in books about relationships, but couples therapy is tailored to the specific needs of you and your partner. Okay, I'm stepping off my soapbox now.

After the first miscarriage, during a particularly long and vulnerable conversation, Michael asked if I would be interested in couples therapy. I was surprised by this offer because couples therapy is something Michael had previously shied away from. His offering made me feel that he truly understood the depth of my grief and the impact it had on me and our relationship. There were so many reasons for us to go to couples therapy during this time. We needed to process our loss, including our individual and joint reactions, and we wanted to figure out how to best support each other. Also, while we both wanted children, we had a lot of fears about another miscarriage, and worries that children may not be in our future, at least not in the ways we expected. Additionally, we had begun exploring the very real possibility of a future without children. Couples therapy was the perfect place to explore all of these concerns.

During our sessions, our therapist gently helped us explore the feelings of grief and sadness we were experiencing. Additionally, he helped me dig into the feelings of disappointment and hurt I had felt at Michael's initial reaction, and guided me in expressing these

72

emotions to Michael while also assisting him in hearing my reaction and expressing his own sense of confusion and loss after the miscarriage. John was a freaking magician.

I mentioned earlier that there is no playbook for how to respond to or support your partner after a miscarriage or any kind of significant loss. While that is true, it can be so helpful having a trained professional in the room helping you navigate these painful conversations. John did not have the definitive answers on how to best support each other or how we were "supposed" to act, but he did offer us space and permission to intentionally explore and identify our grief. Attending those sessions allowed us to feel like we were taking a proactive step for our relationship.

You know that clichéd saying "This can either make or break you." Well, when it comes to your relationship after miscarriage, this statement has a kernel of truth in it. Research suggests that relationship satisfaction can significantly decline after pregnancy loss, and that couples are at a higher risk for separation.[14] Author Kristen Swanson, a professor of family and child studies and lead author on a study on women's perceptions on the effects of miscarriage on their relationships,[15] writes, "When miscarriage affects couples it may stimulate growth, or unearth the inability to support each other through troubled times."[16]

---

[14] Shreffler, K. M., Hill, P. W., & Cacciatore, J., "Explaining Increased Odds of Divorce Following Miscarriage or Stillbirth," Journal of Divorce and Remarriage, no. 53 (2012): 91–107.

[15] Swanson, Kristen M., RN, PhD, FAAN, Zahra A. Karmali, BA, Suzanne H. Powell, BS, BA and Faina Pulvermakher, BS, MT (ASCP), "Miscarriage Effects on Couples' Interpersonal and Sexual Relationships During the First Year After Loss: Women's Perceptions," Psychosomatic Medicine no. 65 (2003): 902-910.

[16] Allen, Colin, "How Couples Fare After Miscarriage," Psychology Today, October 1, 2003, https://www.psychologytoday.com/us/articles/200310/how-couples-fare-after-miscarriage.

Thus, taking proactive steps for your relationship, whether it is through couples therapy, intentional conversations about your grief, or whatever support suits your relationship, can make a world of difference for years to come.

Exercise: Let's Talk About It

When you and your partner are feeling connected, find a comfortable space and time to explore the following ten questions. When you are sharing your responses, try to use I-statements, express what you need versus what you don't need, and stick to describing your own experiences, feelings, and needs. When you are listening to your partner, tune into your partner's feelings, respond with validation and compassion, and ask open-ended questions to better understand your partner and to encourage them to explore further.

- What has been your experience of our miscarriage?
- What have you learned about me after our miscarriage?
- What have you learned about yourself?
- What have you learned about our relationship?
- How has our miscarriage affected your desire for intimacy (in all forms)?
- What have I done after our loss that you have found helpful?
- What can I do to support you further?
- How has our loss impacted your priorities for our relationship?
- How has our loss impacted your individual priorities for your life, career, and goals?
- How has our loss impacted your feelings about starting a family?

Chapter 6
GRIEF AFTER A MISCARRIAGE.
IT'S A THING.

Disclaimer

Warning: This chapter is sad as fuck. This may not come as much of a surprise for a chapter that starts with "Grief," but remember, you've been warned.

While I cried while writing many parts of this book, this one was like the Niagara Falls of crying. This chapter touches on some of the particularly painful aspects of grieving after a miscarriage. It acknowledges the wounds of pregnancy loss that are rarely given space. I encourage you to reach for some support during as well as after this chapter, and if you're like me, some good ol' shower crying time.

Disenfranchised Grief

The grieving of a miscarriage is a complicated, painful, and often confusing process. While grieving the loss of your child, you are also mourning the dreams, hopes, and desires you had for your child that never got to be born. Additionally, while dialogue around pregnancy loss is slowly increasing, there is a lack of understanding in our culture in how to respond to it. The grief following a miscarriage falls into the category of what's referred to as *disenfranchised grief*, or grief that is not openly acknowledged by society, socially accepted, or publicly mourned.[17] This often happens when our relationship to

---

[17] Lang, A., Fleiszer, A. R., Duhamel, F., Sword, W., Gilbert, K. R.,

the deceased is one that society deems as too distant or somehow not worthy of grief. Other losses that fall into this category include the loss of an ex-spouse or infertility

The impact of disenfranchised grief is that it can cause you to doubt whether you are entitled to your grief. If society does not count this as a "real" loss, how can I? I certainly faced this experience myself as those in my community questioned the validity of my loss through statements such as "There wasn't a baby anyway, right?" While I am sure that these individuals did not intend to invalidate my grief, it was statements like these that made me question whether I was entitled to grieve. Were my losses worthy of the sadness, devastation, and pain that I felt? Fortunately, through my training and through reassurance from my loved ones, I was able to acknowledge that yes, this loss is so painfully real and worthy of grieving.

While I am fortunate enough to work in a practice that would have allowed me to take additional time off if needed, I recognize that this is a luxury that most individuals are not given. Maybe we can take time off if we are getting a D&C or need time to heal from the physical effects of a miscarriage, but there is typically no family or medical leave offered after miscarriage. This too can send the message that there is only a certain amount of time you should feel upset after a miscarriage and that you are expected to return to work, fully functioning, after just a couple of days (if that).

As a society, we are ill-prepared to respond to grief and to support those around us who have experienced loss, really any kind of loss. Death of a loved one and the

---

& Corsini-Munt, S., "Perinatal Loss and Parental Grief: The Challenge of Ambiguity and Disenfranchised Grief," OMEGA, no. 63 (20122): 183–196.

subsequent grief that follows is a universally human experience. And yet, even though we will all experience grief at some point in our lives, there is little formal or informal recognition of the impact of loss.

Incomplete Grief

Apart from the invalidation and pain caused by disenfranchised grief, there are dangers in not allowing individuals to fully grieve their loss. Incomplete grief occurs when internal or external factors prevent us from fully acknowledging and healing from a loss. Internal barriers could include focusing on the needs of others to avoid experiencing your own painful feelings and reactions, while external barriers could be a lack of time or space to fully process your loss due to work or family obligations. Signs that may suggest you are experiencing incomplete grief include:

- Uncharacteristic irritability and/or anger.
- Hypervigilance and fear of more loss. After a loss, life can feel more fragile, and individuals may start to consistently scan their environment waiting for the next tragedy to strike.
- Relational changes. After a loss, individuals may cling more tightly to their loved ones for fear of losing them, or some may swing to the other side, distancing themselves from others to protect themselves from further pain.
- Addictive or self-harming behaviors. To distract or numb themselves from pain, individuals may start engaging in risky or harmful behavior such as over-drinking, binge-eating, or workaholism.[18]

---

[18] Krosch, Daniel Jay, and Jane Shakespeare-Finch, "Grief, Traumatic Stress, and Posttraumatic Growth in Women Who Have Experienced Pregnancy Loss," *Psychological Trauma: Theory, Research, Practice, and Policy* no. 9.4 (2017): 425.

What is the alternative to incomplete grief? Grief recovery. In The Grief Recovery Handbook, authors John James and Russell Friedman define grief recovery as the process of being able to fully acknowledge, reflect, and process one's loss.[19] It means giving yourself permission to feel a full range of emotions, from sadness towards what has been lost to joy when reflecting on past fond memories. Grief recovery means waking up one day and realizing that your ability to talk about your loss is normal and healthy. This process involves a series of small choices, including intentionally reflecting on what has been lost, starting with...

Grieving a Dream

We grieve the loved ones who have died because of our attachment to them, because we loved them, because we cared deeply about them. Similarly, we grieve a miscarriage because we have lost a child that many of us have already become strongly attached to, and we grieve a dream that no longer will come to fruition. I remember wondering during my "Should I really be this devastated?" phase shortly after my first miscarriage, if it was possible to grieve someone you never got to know. James and Russel discuss this very idea and describe how we become attached to a dream, belief, and/or idea in the same way we get attached to a person.

I had imagined a whole lifetime of memories of my future child. I thought of the trips we would take together, the family she would get to be a part of, her first day of

---

[19] James, John and Russell Friedman, The Grief Recovery Handbook: The Action Program for Moving Beyond Death, Divorce, and Other Losses including Health, Career, and Faith (New York: HarperColins

school, her first lost tooth, the day she'd learn to ride a bike—I saw all the details so clearly. I even fantasized about Michael and me being sleep-deprived parents who felt like zombies, but who were emotionally fuller than we had ever been. I mourn my two miscarriages, and I mourn the dreams that I had for each future child.

Consider the dreams you had for your baby. Reflect on them, acknowledge the pain of losing them. It causes me pain even as I write this to accept that those beautiful dreams are no longer a possibility. And while it is so painful to think about, taking the time to reflect on the loss of not only your child, but the dreams you held for him or her, is a necessary step in our grieving process.

Mourning the First Pregnancy You'll Never Get to Have

Another part of this loss that deserves some attention is the grieving of your first experience of pregnancy. This will only be true for some who have experienced a miscarriage, but for myself, my first miscarriage was also my first pregnancy. It was my first experience of seeing that positive come up when I peed on the stick (and then seeing that positive come up eight more times as I continued to spend way too much money on pregnancy tests). It was my first experience of seeing my husband's eyes light up when I told him we were going to be parents and to feel his excitement when he held me close. There were so many exhilarating firsts during the weeks after my positive pregnancy test, including telling my family, telling my close friends, and telling my colleagues. After we found out about the miscarriage, a thought came to my mind that I don't think I would have considered had I not been in this situation: I will never have the first pregnancy I wanted. I

Publisher, 2017).

will never get to have the joyous and exciting first pregnancy experience with my husband where we just get to stay excited and happy and share our joy with our loved ones.

Why is this important, you ask? Good question. I know a few loved ones didn't seem to understand my concerns when I shared my grief over losing my chance at a first successful pregnancy. I explained it like this. Let's say (let's hope), Michael and I get pregnant again. I know there will be excitement and joy, but there will also be anxiety and caution—so much caution. There won't be a carefree, blissfully ignorant experience of pregnancy focused on joyful anticipation. And that certainly did prove to be the case with my second pregnancy, which also ended in a miscarriage.

I almost imagine it as when you're a kid, you hear the bumps in the night and you get scared. Your parents tell you everything is going to be okay, there is no boogeyman waiting in the closet. You can sleep safely knowing that everything is okay and the boogeyman will never exist for you outside of your nightmares. After a miscarriage, however, you learn the boogeyman is real, and there is no way to unknow that. When I experience the inevitable bumps in the night (i.e., the fears, the anxieties, the long list of what-ifs), I won't be able to tell myself the boogeyman isn't real because I've come face to face with him and experienced his terror. (See Chapter 10 in how to cope with fears of pregnancy after miscarriage.)

So, I'm pissed. I'm angry and I'm full of rage that I don't get to have that blissfully happy and relatively easy first pregnancy. I grieve for myself and for all of those women who do not get to have the unfettered joy we were promised. If I get pregnant again, I will be excited, but so very cautious in my excitement, and I grieve for myself and for you, dear reader, that we will not have the unencumbered joy we may have had before our miscarriages.

Loss of a Part of Your Identity

This may not be true for all of you, but for those whose miscarriage was also their first pregnancy (as opposed to women who already have children and then experience a miscarriage) you may experience a loss of part of your identity.[20] As previously discussed, the moment that pregnancy test turns positive, you start to see the world through new lens. You become protective and careful. You start to wonder about the hygiene of your favorite hole-in-the-wall Malaysian restaurant, you pore over ingredient lists, on the lookout for chemicals and carcinogens, and you worry about all the hidden dangers in the world, such as suddenly falling down the stairs or contracting salmonella. You start to see the world as a mother.

And then just as you're getting used to this new way of seeing the world, your membership in the motherhood club is cruelly revoked. All at once there is a cosmic shift in your perspective of the world and your sense of identity. You are no longer a mother-to-be, but once again "just" a woman. It's startling, it's sudden, and it is another loss to be acknowledged.

Debunking the Five Stages of Grief

There are several psychological concepts so well-known that almost anyone in the general public would be able to identify them, including Freud's psychosexual theories, the

---

[20] Toller, P. W., "Bereaved Parents' Negotiation of Identity Following the Death of a Child," *Communications Studies*, no. *59* (2008): 306–321.

belief that we can blame our parents for most of our adult trials and tribulations, and the five stages of grief. The five stages of grief were created by Elizabeth Kubler-Ross, a psychiatrist and expert on dying and death. They include depression, anger, bargaining, denial, and acceptance.[21] Through her work, Kubler-Ross was able to make some ground-breaking insights into how we experience death, and reduce the stigma in discussing the universal experience of loss.

However, what you may not know is that Kubler-Ross didn't originally develop these stages to explain what people go through when they lose a loved one. Instead, she developed them to describe the process patients go through as they confront their diagnoses of a terminal illness. The stages were only later applied to the experience of those who have lost a loved one, who seemed to undergo a similar process after their loss. Unfortunately, I imagine as most of us know from personal experience, grief is not that simple. Kubler-Ross has since stated that she regrets publishing her research on grief, as it has led to the belief that there is a prescriptive or "correct" way of grieving after loss.[22] While there may be some overlap between the experiences of those who are facing death and those who have faced death in loss, this model has its limitations and its consequences.

I've had clients who are grieving all different types of loss who have attempted to label the stage they are in and have tried to push themselves to enter the next "correct" phase. Such as, "Well, I've been angry and sad. Now, I

---

[21] Kübler-Ross, Elisabeth, and David Kessler, *On Grief and Grieving: Finding the Meaning of Grief Through the Five Stages of Loss* (New York: Simon and Schuster, 2005).

[22] Stroebe, Margaret, Henk Schut, and Kathrin Boerner, "Cautioning Health-Care Professionals: Bereaved Persons are Misguided Through the Stages of Grief," OMEGA-Journal of Death and Dying no. 74.4 (2017): 455-473.

need to move towards acceptance." I will say it again, there is no correct or sequential process of grief. For some, there may be stages Kubler-Ross did not mention, and there may be some stages we skip altogether. The truth of my miscarriage was too real, too visceral, for me to experience denial. (In fact I wished for a little denial – sounds like it would have been a pleasant break.) And I felt too helpless and devastated to consider what bargaining would even look like in this situation. Of course, if you experience feelings of denial or bargaining – that's completely okay! The point here is that we need to rid ourselves of the expectation that there are certain stages or psychological dilemmas that we will need to face in order to be healed and that there is a sequential process when it comes to grief. The process is anything but linear and more resembles an emotional roller coaster with zigs and zags, loop-di-loops, and precipitous drops. Or a flaming fucking dumpster fire.

Other Myths about Grief that Need Debunking

As a society, we are ill-prepared to face loss. We are taught throughout our lives how to acquire things but are given no guidance in how to deal when we lose them. Consequently, there are many faulty, incorrect, and just plain harmful myths out there about how we should deal with loss.

Myth #1: Don't feel bad. While sometimes people may say this explicitly, they may also share this sentiment in more subtle ways. For example, a nurse telling me that I shouldn't cry after my miscarriage because "God has a plan for you" was another version of telling me "Don't feel bad" and probably "Can you pull yourself together because I'm getting uncomfortable."

Truth: You will feel bad. You will feel all sorts of bad, including pain, sadness, devastation, anger, the whole gamut of bad. And that is okay. It is okay not to be okay.

Myth #2: Replace the loss. This one is particularly relevant. I had a few well-meaning friends whose response when I shared my grief was "Well, when are you going to try again?" Then after my second miscarriage, when trying again seemed less viable, I heard: "Well, why don't you just adopt?" First, there is no "just" when it comes to adopting, but I'll leave that rant for another time. With both of these statements, the message is: your loss is replaceable and you need to move on.

Truth: Whether I take any of these steps, the loss of my children will always be a part of my story and my family. There is no replacing what has been lost. Michael and I have lost two pregnancies and that is devastating, and I will not shy away from that truth.

Myth #3: Time heals all wounds. This is probably one of the most touted clichés about grief that is complete and utter BS. Think about it like this: if you broke your arm, would you just keep walking around as if everything is normal with the assumption of, "Just need to give it a few weeks and all will be okay." No! No.

Truth: It's not that time heals all wounds, it's what you do with that time that leads to healing. Back to our broken arm example: it's going to the doctor, getting an x-ray, wearing a cast for eight weeks, and living a life that is not normal for a while that leads to healing. Similarly, time alone does not heal the grief from a miscarriage, it's what you do with that time.

Myth #4: Miscarriage grief is related to how long you have been pregnant. I have had two first-trimester miscarriages and received comments such as, "Well, at least it happened early" and "You weren't too attached to it yet, right?"

Truth: Research has shown no association between the length of pregnancy and subsequent grief experienced by a woman. A woman who lost her child at five weeks may be just as devastated as a woman who lost her child at 23 weeks.

Myth #5: Miscarriage grief is related to how long you have been trying. If you just started trying, you won't be as devastated as someone who has been trying for years.

Truth: Why do we have such a need to compare and quantify our grief, people? Physician and author of Unsung Lullabies: Coping with Infertility and Loss[23], Dr. Janet Jaffe, writes, "No matter how far along you were, when a pregnancy fails, you lose a part of your reproductive story. You have experienced a reproductive trauma."[24] I was able to get pregnant pretty quickly both times we tried, and yet was still devastated by both of my miscarriages. There are no set standards when it comes to how we respond to grief.

Grief Comes in Waves

As I've gotten older, I've learned that the seemingly clichéd euphemisms I used to scoff at are often acutely accurate. This holds so true for the idea that "grief comes in waves." Imagine you are on a ship and that ship wrecks and you start drowning, crying for help, trying to hang on to anything that will give you some stability while you frantically fight to stay afloat. Maybe it is a person, maybe it is your pet, or maybe it is something intangible like your passions or life purpose that serve as your proverbial life

[23] Diamond, Martha, David Diamond, and Janet Jaffe, Unsung Lullabies: Understanding and Coping with Infertility (London: St. Martin's Griffin, 2005).
[24] Kersting, Anette, and Birgit Wagner, "Complicated Grief after Perinatal Loss," Dialogues in Clinical Neuroscience vol. 14:2 (2012): 187-94.

preserver. And even if your head makes it above water, it is still so exhausting, scary, and overwhelming. This is your initial experience following a miscarriage.

In the beginning, the sea is so unforgiving, and you keep getting pummeled by gigantic wave after wave to the point where you begin to wonder, will I ever be able to rest? Will I ever be okay? Eventually, in a few days, perhaps a few weeks or months, the waves start to slow down. Certain triggers such as hearing about another friend's healthy pregnancy, being asked by unknowing loved ones about when you will start your family, and reaching milestones such as what would have been your due date or your child's birthday may bring the waves crashing back on you again. You never know what is going to trigger that next tidal wave. But in between all the waves, there is life. There is respite and calm seas and a blue sky. You try so hard to cling onto those moments of tranquility before the next wave arrives.

Sometime in the future, and it varies for everyone, you find that the waves have become a tiny bit smaller and that you can start to predict their arrival. You prepare yourself by reaching out for support, and even though those waves still hurt when they crash into you, you know you can survive them now. You may have scars, you may continue to wonder when the next wave will hit, but you know you will survive them.

The days following my first miscarriage, I felt as if I was drowning. I had never experienced pain and despair in such depths, and while I would cling to the support of Michael and loved ones to keep me afloat, I still dreaded each gigantic wave of grief that hit me. I especially hated the ones that took me by my surprise, such as the sudden grief I felt at living in our "starter house" for over a year without our starter family. Over time, while these waves always hurt, I slowly became surer that I could handle each subsequent crest. That I could ask for support if I needed it, that I could cry if I wanted to, and that I could be angry that the waves wouldn't stop. Soon, I stopped fighting the waves and instead allowed myself to feel the pain and through this step, I was able to acknowledge that I was feeling this pain because of love. I loved the babies that had started growing inside me so much that any reminder of them caused me to grieve. Making space for both my sadness and my love is what eventually has kept me afloat.

Memorializing Your Loss

If you are like me, you may have this yearning to do something with your feelings – to take some sort of action or intentionally express them in some way. I have included an exercise below based on just that intention but want to spend some time considering other ways of memorializing your loss. Depending on your specific experiences and phase of pregnancy, you may have had a memorial or funeral for your baby, but that's not always possible and not for everyone. There are other ways we can say goodbye, such as planting flowers in memory of your unborn child. Gladiolus flowers symbolize remembrance, or you could choose anything that has special meaning to you. Additionally, we can look to other cultures that have specific rituals or traditions when it comes to honoring pregnancy loss. For example, there is a beautiful Buddhist practice called *mizuko kuyo*, a memorial service for anyone who has experienced pregnancy loss or stillbirth.[25] Again, there is no "right" step to memorialize your loss, but if you are needing that, consider a place or an object that had

---

[25] Boland, Jeanne M., "Worlds of Loss: A Review of Narratives of Sorrow and Dignity: Japanese Women, Pregnancy Loss, and Modern Rituals of Grieving by Bardwell L. Smith," *Death Studies* no. 39:1 (2014): 56-57.

special significance for your pregnancy and consider building a memorial around that.

For Michael and me, we planted Gladiolus flowers in our backyard and read our goodbye letters out loud. (I'll describe this practice just below.) Before those flowers inevitably died, because we are terrible gardeners, Michael drew a beautiful picture of two branches symbolizing each of our miscarriages. Months later, I used Michael's drawing as a template for a tattoo I now have on my back of two Gladiolus flowers intersected together (I made sure to wait a few months after my second miscarriage before I took this permanent step).

Exercise: Goodbye Letter

When you feel ready, write a letter to your unborn child. If you have had more than one loss, consider writing different letters for each child, or write one letter that is meant for all your losses. Include your wishes and dreams for your child, your regrets, and your goodbyes. I have shared my letter that I wrote after my first miscarriage as reference.

Dear my first child,

I never said it out loud, but I called you little seed in my head. While the time you grew in me only spanned months, the dreams I had for you went on for years. I dreamed of the big things like Christmas mornings, birthdays, and family vacations, but mostly I dreamed of the small things that I couldn't wait for like rocking you in a chair, seeing you fall asleep on your dad's chest, and just staring into your eyes in absolute wonder that you exist and we get to be your parents. Even the hard things like sleepless nights, endless diaper changes, and spit-up filled my daydreams because those things all meant that we got to have you. Your dad and I spent so much time wondering whether you would be a boy or a girl, whether you would have his blue eyes or my black hair, his confidence or my zany sense of humor (I hoped you had both!). Oh little seed, we already loved you so much. It hurts knowing we will never get to meet you and I regret not savoring the time you lived in me because I was consumed with so much fear to love you. I regret all the people that you won't get to meet. Not just me and your dad, but your grandparents, aunts, and uncles. They were all so ready to meet you. I so wish there was something I could have done to give you a life. I truly would have given you anything. I'm sorry you didn't get that chance at life. You deserved it and I promise to love you always. I want to say goodbye to you and I want to promise that you will always have your dad and me. You will always have a family.

Love,

Your mom

Chapter 7

YOUR RELATIONSHIP WITH YOUR BODY AFTER MISCARRIAGE: IT'S COMPLICATED

If I had to define my relationship status with my body before miscarriage, I would say "In a relationship" and happily so. I've always been an active person and frequently pushed myself to extremes through marathons and playing competitive tennis for years. Additionally, I am the biggest proponent of play and always have been. Give me something with wheels and I'm all over it. I'm talking bikes, skateboards, scooters (electric and not), rollerblades, and rip sticks. My standard was if it's the toy of choice for a 12-year-old boy, it's good enough for me. The world has always been my playground and I have taken full advantage of my body to explore it. The consequence of this kind of adventurous living was seven broken bones, 68 stitches on my forehead, and a number of other injuries over the years that left my parents with perpetual heart palpitations and, as I got older, left me with expensive hospital bills. But in my mind it was all worth it, and I engaged in this kind of play right up to my first pregnancy. In fact, I had been playing around on an electric skateboard the weekend before I found out I was pregnant the first time.

During pregnancy, my relationship with my body changed dramatically. I no longer took the sort of risks I had in the past. I avoided anything with wheels (apart from my car) and no longer approached the world like it was my playground. I wouldn't even bike! I remember I had a work trip in the Texas hill country shortly after I found out I was pregnant. At some point, a few of us went out to explore the beautiful lake in front of our cabin. Everyone started climbing down the small hillside to reach the lake below. Before pregnancy I would have been leading this expedition, reveling in the steep descent and the jumps you had to make from boulder to boulder. Pregnant me approached this experience very differently. I was cautious where I used to be brave, I was hesitant where I used to be impulsive, and I paused when I used to jump. This way of approaching the world felt foreign to me, but I embraced it because my number-one priority was no longer myself or my enjoyment, it was protecting the baby growing inside of me.

After my first miscarriage, the status of my relationship with my body changed to "It's complicated" and "I'm debating breaking up with you." And following my second miscarriage, it changed to "Fuck you, body. We are done." While of course there is no way I could literally be "done," I certainly felt disconnected from my body in a way I never had before. This was all new territory for someone who's always been an active person, who reveled in inhabiting a body that has afforded me so many exciting adventures, from rock climbing to running marathons to biking to having amazing sex with my husband. Like I said, we were in a happy relationship!

After my miscarriages, my body no longer felt like my own. Previously, we were a team. My body aided me on all my adventures and fulfilled all my wishes. I wanted to be a mother so badly and I wished to protect that child growing inside of me so acutely. Having a miscarriage—not once but twice—made me feel like my body was letting me down in the worst way possible. How could my mind want something so desperately that my body couldn't deliver?

The team was no longer together.

The Punisher

As mentioned in a previous chapter, I passed out from a nicotine overdose after my first miscarriage was confirmed. After my second miscarriage was confirmed, I drank several beers, and I don't even like beer. In both situations, I was looking for an escape, a distraction from my pain. I also wanted to freely engage in activities that had been denied to me because I was pregnant and eager to protect the fragile human life I already cared so much about. But mostly I smoked hookah to the point of passing out and drank several beers that I did not enjoy because there was a not-so-tiny part of me that wanted to punish my body for miscarrying.

During both my pregnancies, I approached my body with kid gloves and a new kind of care. Pre- pregnancy I would go a whole week without eating any vegetables other than the lettuce and onions on my burger. To be clear, I'm not proud of this behavior. I was just so used to approaching my body through a lens of pleasure versus care. During pregnancy, I made sure that I had a diet that included fruits, vegetables, and plenty of calcium. I made sure to get all the sleep I needed, I drank more water than I ever had before, and I took such care in responding to whatever my body needed. Therapists often have back-to-back sessions with barely 10 minutes in between. Before pregnancy, I'd use those allotted 10 minutes, which were usually closer to five minutes, to write down notes from my previous session and review my notes for my next client. Even if I was hungry or needed to pee, I would wait till my stomach was audibly growling or my bladder felt like it was about to burst before I would take care of myself.

After I was pregnant, I was attuned to my body's

signals in a way I never had been before. I made sure that all my sessions ended with enough time for me to go to the bathroom because I needed to every hour, and to have a snack when I needed to versus waiting until I was so hungry that both my client and I could not ignore my stomach's protests.

After my miscarriages, this doting, attentive behavior abruptly stopped. I went back to my old habits and even a little further, drinking loads of caffeine each day, more alcohol than I should have, and consuming a diet that left me feeling like crap. I felt some sort of strange satisfaction in this behavior. Looking back, I realize a lot of these actions had to do with the lack of control I felt in life, but especially with my body. I never explicitly acknowledged this at the time, but I know my mind had decided that If I had no control over keeping my pregnancy, then at least I had control over what happened to my body after pregnancy. I had decided that by having multiple miscarriages, my body had committed a crime, and punishment was the only response.

Hormonal Rollercoaster

We can't have a chapter about our bodies after a miscarriage without addressing the hormonal dumpster fire that accompanies this journey. Even after a miscarriage, your hCG levels may still be high for weeks to come, meaning that you may continue to experience some of the symptoms of pregnancy, including fatigue and sore breasts. This is one of the more hellish aspects of pregnancy loss in my opinion. Additionally, your mood may be on the wildest rollercoaster ride due to both the hormonal changes and the grief that you are still walking through. I felt like Dr. Jekyll and Mr. Hyde if Dr. Jekyll was moody as hell and Mr. Hyde was the grouchiest and most unpredictable woman you had ever met.

Apart from my mood being all over the place, my body still wore remnants of pregnancy, including breasts that were two cup sizes bigger and the weight I had gained. Michael did an amazing job of reassuring me that I looked amazing, and granted, most heterosexual men would be happy that their partners' breasts had grown two cup sizes almost overnight. I, on the other hand, resented these changes fiercely.

Part of my reaction was that I have been roughly the same height, weight, and bra size since 9th grade. I still remember going to my pediatrician at age 15 and being told, "You've stopped growing." First, what a weird thing to tell someone. Second, how the hell does a doctor make that kind of determination? Third, that arrogant son of a gun was right, and I remained the same height and approximately the same weight and bra size for the next 13 years of my life. And then all of a sudden, in my second pregnancy, I went from a 34B to a 32DD. I was shocked and shared this with all my friends who had experienced pregnancy, who laughingly responded that me and my breasts were in for a wild ride. Given my previous pregnancy, during which my breasts did not double in size, I chose to believe that maybe this was a good sign that this pregnancy was different. So, I bought new D-cup bras from Victoria's Secret and reveled in the new changes. That reveling ended immediately after I learned about my second miscarriage. My D-cup bras now served as harbingers of what I had lost.

Similarly, while I didn't love gaining weight, I acknowledged it as a part of the process of motherhood, and again took it as a sign that my pregnancy was proceeding as it should. Following my first miscarriage, I once complained about my pregnancy weight gain to a friend of mine who had recently given birth, and she attempted to commiserate with me, sharing that she too felt stressed about the weight she had been struggling to lose. While I appreciated the sentiment, the distinction in our situations was clear. We had both gained weight during pregnancy, but her weight gain led to a baby, while mine felt like insult added to injury. I fiercely resented the extra pounds and the differences I noticed in the way my clothes fit, as they served as daily reminders of what I had gone through and what was lost.

Mind-Body Connection

There is a complex interrelationship between our mind and body, and in therapy, I often explore with my clients how their thoughts, feelings, and beliefs can affect their biological states. For example, take me before a presentation. I feel quite anxious, and the thoughts swirling around in my brain vacillate from: "You got this. You are prepared and ready," to "This is going to be awful. Why the fuck do you keep putting yourself in this situation?" As these thoughts get louder and louder, I notice my stomach churning and have to make more frequent stops to the bathroom. Thanks brain, now I'm anxious and my stomach hurts. Conversely, the way we treat our bodies certainly affects our minds. Think about how you feel after a hangover, lack of sleep, or a 3-piece spicy meal from Popeyes. So I often spend time with a client considering how their sleep, diet, alcohol use, and whatever else they consume could affect the way their mind operates.

During pregnancy, this already complicated interrelationship between our mind and our body gets even more complex. Before pregnancy, there seems to be a reciprocal, almost linear relationship between our minds and our bodies. For example, you drink a lot of margaritas one night and then you feel like crap the next day. Well, that rule book is thrown out the window during pregnancy. You can sleep for 10 hours and still feel exhausted. You can eat healthier than you ever have and still feel like you're going to hurl at any moment. Now this can be crazy-making, but somehow it didn't feel that way to me. Yes, I definitely complained about the exhaustion, the food aversions, and the thickness I noticed in my waist. However, each of these changes served as reminders of the baby that was growing inside of me.

After my miscarriages, I didn't know how to view my body. It was certainly no longer a cocoon for growing my child, and I did not want to enlist its aid in play and exploration, even if I was in the mood for either. Often times, my clients share with me their desire to go back to "normal." This desire to return to baseline is completely understandable. As humans, we are hardwired to find a place of homeostasis, stability in our system. However, the unfortunate truth that I share with my clients is that we can't go back to that old normal because we can't erase the physical or emotional impact that rocked our system in the first place. Instead, we have to create a "new normal."

As much as I wanted to at times, I couldn't erase the indelible imprint that my miscarriages had on my body and my mind. I had an increased awareness of my body and what it was capable of outside of play and pleasure. It took me months, but I finally started to reconcile the relationship between my body and my mind. I realized that I had taken so much of what my body could do for me for granted. I gave it so little care when it had given so much to me over the years. My new normal meant that I still prioritized play and pleasure in my life, but I also made room for nourishment and care. Y'all, I kept eating vegetables and fruits! This may not seem like a big deal to most functioning adults, but for me it was a lifestyle change and more importantly it was a homage to my amazing body.

98

Forgiving your Body

I need to embrace some irony here. As I am writing this section about our relationship with our bodies, I noticed myself getting super frustrated with my body. Here is the backstory. About a week ago, I broke my pinky finger catching a football. Turns out you are supposed to keep your fingers wide when you're catching the ball, not in a claw-like shape, which can easily result in your finger getting jammed. You live and you learn. I learned that a bone in my pinky finger had shattered into four pieces. All that to say, I noticed myself getting so irritated as I was writing this chapter, as my left hand is barely functional due to the splint I must wear for the next month.

Typically, when I'm writing, my hands keep pace with the flow of my thoughts. If I'm in the zone, I can write 2,500 words in 40 minutes. Now I have to slow things down, correct the dictation software I'm using, and I find myself thinking "Ugh, I hate you, stupid hand." I also may have screamed it out loud a few times.

It took me a few paragraphs, but I finally realized the parallel. Here I am again berating my body for not functioning the way I want it to! And here I am again reminding myself of everything that my body can do and everything it allows me to do. Yes, I have a broken pinky finger and typing is slower than I would like it to be, but I also did a kickboxing workout this morning and I had fabulous sex with my husband last night.

I don't know if my body will ever be able to have a successful pregnancy, but I do know it's capable of so many other things that I often take for granted. So, dear readers, please take a second and acknowledge all that your body does for you and consider what kind of care you show it. In that acknowledgment, make space for sadness and disappointment and also make space for gratitude and joy. Yes, I am devastated for the loss of my pregnancies and I'm grateful for all that my body can do. Yes, I am irritated by my broken pinky finger and I'm grateful that I still caught that football.

Exercise: Show that Body Some Love

For the next week, I want to challenge you to pay special attention to what your body allows you to do and then identify a way to express your gratitude to your body. This can be as simple as saying "Thank you, body" after a workout, after some great sex, after a great meal, or after anything that your body has allowed you to do. You can also consider treating or luxuriating in your body in some way. For example, I have always rushed through my after-shower routine, quickly slathering on my moisturizer and lotion while watching Netflix on my phone. After my body and I decided to make up, I treated myself to some decadent lotion that I use mindfully while reflecting on everything my body allowed me to do that day.

What can you do to show your body some care? I have listed a few suggestions below:

- Intentionally thank your body for how it serves you
- Take bubble baths
- Treat yourself to some fancy lotion or moisturizer and apply it slowly and thoughtfully
- Get a massage
- Do a workout you love

Chapter 8
NOT TODAY, SHAME

Through my years as a psychologist, I have become well equipped in helping individuals uncover the devastating, humiliating, and painful feeling that is shame. Shame is that uncomfortable feeling we experience when we not only feel we have done something bad, but that we *are* bad. Wholly different from the temporary embarrassment you feel at making a mistake or the guilt you feel at forgetting a friend's birthday, shame is a much bigger, badder animal. Guilt says "I made a mistake" while shame says "I *am* the mistake." The link between shame and miscarriage has been backed by countless studies and is one of the main reasons individuals who've suffered pregnancy loss stay silent.[26]

Similar to many other emotional landmines, I was completely aware of the impact of shame on one's psyche, but that in no way made me invulnerable to its effects. Brené Brown uses the term "shame gremlins" to describe those recurring stories our minds tell us about how we are somehow deficient or not worthy. She discusses how beneficial it can be to become familiar with the specific tracks our shame gremlins like to play on repeat.[27] I certainly had a few tracks that would just not stop playing, including...

---

[26] Barr, P., "Guilt- and Shame-Proneness and the Grief of Perinatal Bereavement," *Psychology and psychotherapy: Theory, Research and Practice* no. 77, (2004): 493–510.
[27] Brown, Brené, "Shame Resilience Theory: A Grounded Theory Study on Women and Shame," Families in Society no. 87.1 (2006): 43-52.

I Failed in my Wifely Duties.

Will my in-laws be mad that I can't bear a child for my husband? That feels like such an archaic, ridiculous statement to write, but that question went through my mind so many times after our miscarriage. I wondered if my in-laws would think that Michael had married the wrong person, and that if he had ended up with an Indiana Hoosier instead of an Asian Texan, he would already have a brood of children. This thought felt positively medieval, bringing to mind images of some 16th century version of ourselves, my in-laws disgruntled that we hadn't provided a child to work on the family farm and the villagers casting disapproving glances at the "barren" woman in their midst. Clearly, none of these thoughts were rational or based on reality—and they brought about their own sense of shame—but that's the way shame works. It distorts our thinking and gives us tunnel vision. Instead of being able to step back and recognize all the love, compassion, and support my in-laws had always shown me and continued to show me after our miscarriages, all I could focus on was the fact that I had not provided them with the child they all wanted and would be found lacking as a result.

I'm Less of a Woman.

Another track that seemed to be playing on repeat was the idea that because I could not have a child, I was somehow less of a woman. We are shown this narrative again and again in movies, books, and in our daily lives that women fall in love, get married, and then have children (sometimes not in that order, which just adds some unique flavor to the story, but they always end up with that baby). Well, I had step one and step two down, but couldn't quite complete step three. I was a 29-year-old married woman, established in my career, living in suburbia...and not producing any children. I was not fulfilling the womanly narrative that I had seen play out hundreds of times—not to mention a narrative my best friends were all playing out brilliantly. It felt like not only was I doing something wrong, I *was* something wrong.

There seems to be this indelible association between being a woman and being a mother. Once a woman reaches a certain age, there is a general assumption that she will soon have a child. That's why people ask all those lovely, terrible questions about when is it going to be my turn to have a baby? And why I too was guilty of asking people those questions in the past, because I just assumed that's what happens, that is the way the story goes. So yes, I too succumbed to the "less of a woman" fallacy: what was wrong with me and my body that I could not get this essential, identity-defining step of womanhood right?

I Shouldn't Be this Sad

When it comes to the recovery process after a miscarriage, there is truly no comparison between people—we all experience and process grief so differently. One of my friends, while certainly upset after her miscarriage, said the worst of it was behind her within a few months and she then went on with life as usual. Another friend shared that her miscarriage continued to impact her even years later, and while I could hear and acknowledge her experience, somehow I could not allow myself the same freedom to experience my feelings following my first pregnancy loss.

Some of the first thoughts that plagued me then were "Why am I so sad?" and "What is wrong with me that I cannot get over this and stop crying?" The "I shouldn't be this sad" track got a lot of airtime. Even as I knew there was no use to this line of thinking and that it was really quite harmful to compare my grief to others, I still weighed my reactions against the reactions of my husband, against my friends who had experienced a miscarriage, and against all the well-wishing people who told us they too had experienced a miscarriage but now had a healthy child and were so happy and complete. This comparison, as you can imagine, just compounded my grief as I was now feeling sadness and devastation as well as shame for being so weak that I was allowing myself to be so affected by my miscarriage.

Exposing the Shame Gremlins

Those were just a few of the tracks playing on repeat after my miscarriages. Fortunately, for both you and me, there is a way to tackle these shame gremlins. Brené Brown uses the analogy from the *Gremlins* movie that when the gremlins were exposed to light, they were destroyed. Similarly, when I felt brave and supported enough to share my "shame tracks" with Michael or loved ones, I noticed that the power of these statements soon faded. For example, for weeks I sat with the track that told me my in-laws were going to hate me because I could not have a child. This track went dormant during my second pregnancy, but then reared its ugly head all over again after my second miscarriage.

After living with this story in my mind for months, I finally shared it with my husband as we were driving home after my second D&C. "Do you think your family is going to hate me for not being able to have kids?" I asked. Michael, because he is amazing, did not immediately laugh or dismiss my question, but instead asked where this thought was coming from. As I began to explain it, I experienced Brown's theory coming to life: as I exposed my shame gremlin to the light, I became aware of how ludicrous this story sounded. I didn't criticize myself for having this story in my head, but allowed myself to really hear the inaccuracy of it while experiencing the love and support of Michael.

And just like that, the track that had consumed hours of my time and so much energy evaporated.

The Power of Noticing and Naming

If there was one technique I could teach someone in therapy, it would be the exercise of noticing and naming. It is SO impactful to be able to become aware of the stories our mind tells us, and this is certainly the case for our shame gremlins. While the intensity of my shame tracks decreased when I exposed them to the light and the support of my loved ones, they still popped up every now and again. This is where noticing and naming comes in. Let's say my sister-in-law shares how excited she is for us to have kids one day and just like that my shame gremlin rockets to the surface. Cue the old shame track: "What if I can never have kids? My sister-in-law will probably hate me and wish that Michael had married someone else. I have failed in my wifely duties." Instead of battling against this track, I notice it and I give it a name.

A key part of noticing is that it's done without judgment and self-blame. You simply acknowledge that thought—ah, there you are, I see you—and then you name it. To come up with a name, I will often ask my clients, "If we were to put all the thoughts, images, and feelings of this experience in a book, what would the title be?" The title of the shame track I described above became "My Wifely Duties." Thus, when I notice that particular shame gremlin come up, I simply say, "Ah, My Wifely Duties is popping up" or even "There she is, My Wifely Duties, back for a visit." By allowing it to be acknowledged, with no judgment and even with a glint of humor, the proverbial light zaps the shit out of that shame gremlin.

Why Do We Wait Till the 12-Week Mark?

A discussion about shame does not seem complete without acknowledging the well-known 12-week rule. This rule dictates that couples should wait 12 weeks to reveal a pregnancy to the world. This is based on the research that first trimester miscarriages are relatively common. In fact, one in four pregnancies will end in miscarriage. The high frequency of miscarriages would make one think it's something we would discuss more often with each other. Instead, the opposite phenomenon occurs. We are told to keep silent for any number of unhelpful (and isolating) reasons: shame, guilt, embarrassment, choose your poison. God forbid we or our partners reveal that we've gone through this painful and relatively common experience. Right? Hell no!

I remember once hearing a friend talk about a mutual acquaintance who had recently had a miscarriage. Instead of sharing her compassion and sorrow regarding this woman's loss, she appeared mildly scandalized and said, "I don't know why she told people so early. It just makes it so awkward." This exchange occurred prior to my first miscarriage and I remember not saying much at the time, but I distinctly recall thinking, "What an odd reaction. Why does it bother you so much?" I have that same reaction now, as well as WHAT THE ACTUAL HELL?! As if it was a personal affront to her that she had to hear this painful news. As if it was more important to focus on the woman sharing her news of pregnancy than the devastation she could be experiencing. To be clear, I'm not looking to vilify this woman. Her reaction is unfortunately all too common and one whose roots go back centuries.

Let's take a look at where this idea of hiding

pregnancy comes from. There are millennia-old beliefs that posit that a women's role in life is to be fruitful and multiply and that women are fulfilling their expected religious and societal duty by becoming mothers. Yet, while this expectation has been placed on women for centuries, the 16th century heralded a time in which women were expected to go into confinement during pregnancy as a "social precaution." Historian Clair Hanson writes, "Social discomfort with the pregnant state was connected with the embarrassment inspired by visible signs of female sexual activity."[28] Thus, for centuries women were expected to produce multiple children for the "greater good," but when they fulfilled this obligation by becoming pregnant, their reward was months of loneliness as they were confined from the general public.

The utter hypocrisy of this belief is baffling, and yet I sometimes question how far we have come from archaic beliefs like pregnancy confinement. While we are not expected to hide the later stages of our pregnancy, we are expected to hide the beginning of our pregnancy to prevent anticipated social discomfort. When before pregnancy was hidden to conceal the fact that "Gasp! This woman who is pregnant must have had sex!" now it's being hidden because "Gasp! This woman who is pregnant may lose her baby and then I will have to experience pain."

We are a society that runs from pain. This is understandable and evolutionary science would tell us that it is in fact adaptive to move away from pain. Yet, it is this avoidance of pain that leads to the creation of implicit (and sometimes explicit) rules like waiting till the 12-week mark to announce a pregnancy. A rule in which women, just like our female ancestors before us, are sentenced to isolation

---

[28] Hanson, Clare, A Cultural History of Pregnancy: Pregnancy, Medicine and Culture, 1750-2000. (London: Palgrave Macmillan UK, 2004).

and disconnection from others for the crime of fulfilling our "societal duty." As I said, the hypocrisy leaves me baffled.

This rule has been getting some more attention lately as many women and their partners are deciding that they don't give a damn about it. They are excited about their pregnancy and they want to share it with the world. Additionally, they assert that if the worst were to happen, they would want the support of their family and friends.

Preach, my friends! I was certainly in this boat for both of my pregnancies. I told my family and close friends as soon as I found out I was pregnant. My rule of thumb was if this was someone I wanted support from, then I told them. Meaning I told my best friends and I told my boss, but I didn't tell my previous coworker I only speak to a couple of times a year. Michael, on the other hand, told almost everyone he'd had more than a five-minute conversation with about both of our pregnancies. And that's okay because that's his story to share and he gets to decide who hears it. We all get to decide how we share our stories.

As discussed previously, we are rarely taught how to respond to grief, depression, anxiety, anger, or really any other "unpleasant" human emotion. The truth is, it is difficult to see others in pain and it is hard as hell to sit with them in that pain without trying to "silver-line" it or fix it. Consequently, we don't tell people about our own pain because what if it makes them uncomfortable? That is the message that I believe the 12-week rule sends. It says don't share your news of pregnancy because having a miscarriage is not something you talk about. It's something you keep to yourself and lock away. What a recipe for shame.

Exercise: Identifying your Shame Gremlins

Shame gremlins are those recurring stories our minds tell us about how we are somehow deficient or not worthy (e.g., I'm less of a woman, I didn't do enough to protect my baby). Explore and identify the recurring tracks your shame gremlins play and record them below.

Track 1: _____

Track 2: _____

Track 3: _____

Track 4: _____

Track 5: _____

After you have identified your dominant tracks, choose a loved one with whom you feel safe and share these tracks out loud with them. Allow yourself to notice your reaction in speaking these stories out loud, and consider the response of your loved one. The next time this track comes up, notice it and name it explicitly.

Chapter 9

HATING PREGNANT PEOPLE AND ALL THINGS BABY

Baby Showers Post-Miscarriage

I was such a dick during my two best friends' joint baby shower. No way to really mince words there. I was just plain obnoxious and not fun to be around. After my first miscarriage, I began dreading this party, while before my miscarriage, I had actually planned to host and organize the whole event. As I mentioned earlier, I had a public breakdown at a Panera and tearfully told my friends that I was unable to plan their baby showers because it was so freaking painful to even imagine doing so. They were so understanding, and the only role I played in helping was sending out the evites (somehow I managed to send them with the wrong day – I swear it wasn't sabotage!) and getting there early to help them set up.

Why did I dread this day so hard? Well, a few reasons. First, while I was relieved I didn't have to plan a baby shower, I felt terribly guilty that my pregnant best friends, both six months along, had to plan their own first baby celebration. While they both assured me repeatedly that they completely understood and actually had given this event so little thought, I couldn't help but feel like I had really let them down. I also felt sad because these were my best friends for more than a decade and we had long ago planned the graduation parties (check), 21st birthdays (check), bachelorette parties (check), and baby showers (no check) that we would one day throw for each other. While not organizing a baby shower was exactly what I needed, I grieved and was saddened by the fact that I would never be able to throw them their first baby shower. And I'm great at throwing parties, so it would have been magical.

Second, it just plain sucked to be at a completely baby-centered event. One of the intentional coping techniques I had been using for the last few months was avoiding all things baby-related. And I mean ALL things. If babies came up in conversation, I would excuse myself, or more likely I would just Irish goodbye the hell out of that conversation. If babies entered the storyline of one of my favorite television shows, it didn't matter how invested I was or what sort of cliffhanger it served up, I would stop watching immediately. Goodbye "Grey's Anatomy." When I went to stores, I would purposefully take the longer route to avoid passing any Babies "R" Us (which bloody hell, seemed ubiquitous at the time), and once I finally got in a store, I'd wander circuitously in order to avoid the baby or maternity sections. Y'all, the avoidance was real. And then came the unavoidable event, my best friends' baby shower, where baby was plastered EVERYWHERE. I couldn't escape it. It was the center of every conversation – as it should have been – and I was miserable.

Third, it just happened to be the day I got my period. (Oh Universe, you are such a riot!) We had been given the green light the month before from my OB that we could start trying again, and while I doubted that we would conceive so quickly, a part of me certainly held out some hope and had this little, irrational desire that if we did get pregnant again quickly, I could just write this miscarriage off as a little blip in our soon-to-be magical story. And then, PERIOD. Fucking period, magically timed for the baby shower.

So here I am surrounded by pregnant people, baby stuff, and baby conversations, and at the same time I'm having cramps and feeling as far from pregnant as you can get. Also, there was no alcohol, which I suppose makes sense at a baby shower, but it really completed the perfect storm of misery.

This is the part where I start acting like a dick. As in any baby shower, there were several games, one in which each guest got three clothespins and if anyone said the word "baby," the person who heard it would get their clothespin, and the lucky guy or gal with the most clothespins wins. Sounds harmless, right? For anyone not in baby-hating mode, I'm sure it was lovely, but for me, it wasn't just pouring salt in the wound, it was pouring bleach, and then acid, and then setting that wound on fire. Thus, my mind said the only way to cope was to be aggressively competitive to an insufferable degree. I made it my mission to obliterate everyone in this game. This was my super healthy form of coping: to become an obnoxious, slight masochistic party guest who purposefully sought out conversations just to get someone to say the word "baby."

It went something like this:

Guest: "Wow, I haven't seen you since the wedding."

Me: "Yeah, time flies. Have you been to one of these lately?"

Guest: "A baby shower? Yeah, actually my sister—"

Me: "You said 'baby'!! Give me your clothespin." (Leaves conversation and approaches someone else).

Guest: "Gosh, I'm just so happy for them."

Me: "Me too. What did you get them?"

Guest: "Oh, um, the baby swaddle thing they wanted. It's just so exciting thinking about—"

Me: "You said 'baby'!! Gimme that!" (Leaves conversation to rinse and repeat with someone outside of earshot).

Just to be clear, no one else at all was taking this game seriously. Everyone else was relaxed and amicable, engaging in humorous chitchat, while I stomped around like a soldier on a mission. When it was time for the winners to be announced, I heard a few people say, "Can we just give her the prize already?" When my name was called, the loudest clapping was from Michael—with the exception of myself. Remember I said I was being obnoxious? I jumped up and applauded myself—I may have let loose a whoop or two—and ran up to claim my $5 Starbucks gift card.

Another layer to this whole debacle is that with the exception of the overly aggressive clothespin-stealing conversations, I spoke almost exclusively to Michael, making zero to minimal effort to socialize with others. I'm sure I seemed stand-offish and maybe even slightly unhinged given my aggressive pursuit in the game, but I knew I was incapable of making small talk, largely because the few conversations I had inevitably included the question "So when are you and Michael going to have kids?"

Yup. The dreaded question. I had been fearing it for a while, and as in nightmares when you can see a threat coming from miles away and you know there is no escape, this one arrived on cue. I envied Michael's directness whenever he was asked that question, as his habit was to simply respond, "We had a miscarriage in November." Damn, that is one effective conversation stopper. While I would've liked to respond that way at the baby shower, my emotions were too raw to say anything baby-related without instantly bursting into tears. And I was feeling a little tired of my public crying. A few times I answered with a non-committal response such as Michael and I were enjoying the "dink" (double income no kids) life and were focusing on our careers, but it all sounded so fake coming out of my mouth.

Finally, when one unlucky woman asked the dreaded question, I responded, "I'm not sure. When are you making your next big life decision? It must be just around the corner!" Taken aback, she responded somewhat shakily, "Well, me and Tom have been talking about marriage for a while, but yeah I'm not sure. A lot of people keeping asking me that." While I don't feel proud, I allowed myself to take a moment of satisfaction in her obvious discomfort and then said, "Isn't it so crazy how we put so much pressure on each other by asking people to constantly define their next life choices? Like when are you getting married, when are you going to have a kid, or when are you going to have another kid? Why is it never just enough to ask about what's currently going on in our life?" She Irish good-byed me and then studiously avoided me for the rest of the event. Good call, really. Between her and all the other people avoiding me because I was annoying as hell during that game, I was given a real wide berth for the remainder of the party.

There were so many cringe-worthy moments, but somehow, I'm not cringing.

Baby showers used to be a normal level unpleasantness for me (i.e., forced social interaction with people I rarely see while playing weird games), but now they are a new form of hell. If you don't go through this phase, I am so happy for you! But if you do, know that it is okay and SO normal. For the weeks, months, perhaps even years following your miscarriage, baby showers may cause you to feel sadness, anger, disappointment, and shame. Quite an emotionally exhausting cocktail – and on top of that, there may not even be real cocktails at these things!

While I can't imagine any way to make baby showers

enjoyable after a miscarriage, there are a few ways to help you cope with this difficult and often painful situation. First, if you feel comfortable, share with your pregnant friend(s) how you are feeling and let them know what you need and what you don't need. I was consumed with so much guilt and worry before I told my friends that I couldn't plan their joint baby shower. I'd already made up a story in my head that my friends were going to think of me as selfish or weak. Yeah, that story was coming straight from my shame gremlins and in no way matched the reality of the situation. My friends were grateful that I shared with them how I was feeling and were completely understanding, and admitted they had been wondering how I was reacting to their pregnancies. They were glad that I had brought up the proverbial elephant in the room (they in no way looked like elephants, mind you, they were beautiful butterflies).

The point I'm making here is that your friends care about you and they want to support you, so let them know how. For me, that meant I would send the invitations for their joint baby shower and would help with decorating and cleaning up, but I left coming up with the baby games and other parts of the party planning to them. Spend some time considering what would make this experience tolerable for you, and if you feel up to it, share these ideas with your friend(s).

Now, in my experience, I was dealing with my two closest friends, who already knew all the details of my miscarriage and my grief. However, if I was going to the baby shower of a relative, friend, or co-worker who I didn't feel comfortable sharing so much with, here are some other possible approaches. First, if it was an option, I would enlist a buddy to be there with me as my support and potentially to play interference for me when questions about "When is it going to be your turn?" came up. If significant others are invited, you could bring your partner, or if you are close with another friend who will be there, consider enlisting her/him as an ally. If this isn't an option, enlist support from the outside. Have a friend you can call on the way there to give you a pep talk before you go in and to help plan an exit strategy (e.g., I'm only going to stay one hour and then I have to leave because of a work obligation or I left my stove on and my house may be burning down). If possible, plan to meet up with your friend or at least plan to speak to them on the phone after the baby shower to share all the feelings, thoughts, and reactions that came up for you. Preferably over a good cocktail or decadent food.

Another option, of course, which may be difficult depending on the circumstances, is simply to decline the invitation. While I couldn't miss my best friends' baby showers, there were some invitations I just had to decline for my own well-being; I knew I wouldn't be able to hold it together. In those situations, if I felt comfortable, I would share the reason with my friend (who was always understanding – I mean what monster wouldn't be?). If I didn't feel comfortable disclosing, I came up with an excuse, sent a gift and a lovely card, and asked if I could take that friend out for lunch, to a manicure, a massage, or whatever, just to let her know I did care about her and wanted to celebrate her even if I couldn't attend her baby shower.

Fertility Privilege

I first heard the term "fertility privilege" when talking with a friend who had also experienced multiple miscarriages. She described that just like any other form of privilege, fertility privilege refers to the special rights, advantages, or immunity granted to a particular group of people. In simpler terms, some people decide they want to have a baby and then nine months later, BAM, they are welcoming their new child into their family. For the fertility privileged, concerns about how many children they want to have, their preferred gender, and preferred spacing between pregnancies are the kinds of decisions they are weighing. For those who do not fall under the veil of fertility privileged, our decisions often become can I afford another round of IVF, can I physically and emotionally handle another loss, and will this ever happen for me?

Many of us, myself included, grew up in families with fertility privilege. My mother had three kids and no miscarriages. My four maternal aunts had eight children between them, all with no miscarriages. Now it is certainly possible that somewhere along the lines, someone had a miscarriage and never shared that due to stigma, cultural norms, or their own preferences for privacy. However, as a child growing up and as an adult, I developed the belief that if I wanted a baby, I just needed to get off birth control and start trying and then BAM, nine months later, we have a new member of our family. This perception of fertility privilege that I thought was guaranteed to me was shattered when I had my miscarriages. Yet, for many others, the fertility privileged, they can continue with the belief that if they want a baby, they can have one. It's as simple as that.

This is not to say we should bash the fertility privileged, but to acknowledge the pain that comes with witnessing so many other women have successful pregnancies while we continue to struggle to have our rainbow babies (i.e., the baby you have after infertility and/or miscarriage(s)). It feels impossible not to ask ourselves, why me? And why do all these other people get to have multiple successful pregnancies while I can't even have one? Enter my feelings of resentment towards the fertility privileged.

Why it's Okay to Hate Pregnant Women

Let's get real here for a second. Since my miscarriage, I have had a barrage of emotions towards pregnant women including anger, sadness, devastation, rage, disappointment, resentment, and yes, HATE. Sometimes a little nugget of shame can get wrapped up in there because, surely, there must be something inherently wrong with me not to feel anything but positivity and good wishes towards these glowing, expectant mothers, right?

Nope! To be perfectly honest, that shame nugget is small and in fact has almost disappeared: it is so natural to have mixed feelings towards pregnant women after having a miscarriage. Also, carrying all these negative feelings is exhausting enough without having to add the burden of guilt and shame.

A core principle of ACT states that the more we try to fight difficult feelings, the more they smother us. ACT offers the analogy of falling into quicksand – the more you struggle, the more you sink. You feel angry, disappointed, and sad, and then you feel angry, disappointed, and sad for having those feelings in the first place. As your difficult emotions grow exponentially larger, your struggle intensifies, and you fall beneath the surface. Dark, I know. Instead, what if we allowed ourselves to turn off that struggle switch and let our uncomfortable emotions be there? To just float on the surface without fighting them and without justifying them.

Essentially, when we keep our struggle switch on, our emotions are stuck, we waste a huge amount of energy and time struggling against them, and we often create even more pain for ourselves as we feel disappointed by our disappointment. Alternatively, if we are able to turn our struggle switch off, our emotions are free to move, we don't waste time or energy fighting against them, and we don't generate any additional difficult emotions to our already full cocktail of pain.

And then, what if we took it one step further and offered ourselves some compassion for having these difficult feelings in the place of judgement or guilt? Research has shown us time and time again that exercising self-compassion has numerous benefits on our mood, resiliency, and overall mental state.[29] I have included an exercise at the end of this chapter to help you turn off the struggle switch and move towards self-compassion.

Stop Kicking the Puppy

Slightly disconcerting phrase, I know, but it provides a helpful illustration. I first heard this concept on Dr. Maria Rothenburger's "Miracles Happen Fertility Podcast." Dr. Rothenburger described how we experience a multitude of emotions following miscarriage, including sadness, disappointment, shame, guilt, and maybe anger towards others who get to have healthy pregnancies while we struggle with loss after loss. She compared our emotional state to the image of an adorable puppy coming up to you wanting attention and comfort. Puppies have little ability to self-regulate and often come to us for comfort, for food, and for a sense of safety. Now, imagine that puppy approaching you because she is upset. She is whimpering softly and sidling up right next to you. How do you react? Well, assuming you are a human and not a robot or sociopath, I'm assuming you pet the puppy and speak to

[29] Yadavaia, James E., Steven C. Hayes, and Roger Vilardaga, "Using Acceptance and Commitment Therapy to Increase Self-Compassion: A Randomized Controlled Trial," *Journal of Contextual Behavioral Science* no. 3.4 (2014): 248-257.

her in a comforting tone. You would never kick the puppy away and tell it to "get over it," "get on with your life," or "shut up."

What I'm asking is for you to give yourself the same compassion, love, and comfort you would offer that puppy. When you start to notice yourself feeling sad, angry, distressed, ashamed, or that delightful mix of all of the above, don't kick yourself when you already down.

So ladies, please, know that it is so understandable that you are having a complicated reaction to pregnant women right now, and that the best thing you can do for yourself is to exercise some acceptance and compassion towards those feelings. You don't need my permission, but just in case you need to hear it, all those dark, angry thoughts you have when you see a pregnant person or hear that a friend is pregnant is SO completely understandable. I want to give you the freedom to express these thoughts and own them by sharing some of my own thoughts that have come up when I have encountered pregnant loved ones, friends, and oh let's not forget, the multitude of social media pregnancy announcements. Prepare yourself to take a walk on the dark side:

- Why do you get to have four kids when I can't even have one?
- Why do you get to have a healthy, first pregnancy when mine was a nightmare?
- Hearing you complain about all the appointments you have to go to see your healthy, growing baby makes me want to punch you.
- Hearing you complain about how much your baby is kicking you makes me want to kick you, too.
- Hearing you complain about how big you feel about your growing belly that is evidence of your healthy pregnancy, when I didn't get to have one, makes me want to throw things at you.
- To all those women on shows like "16 and Pregnant"

and "I Didn't Know I was Pregnant" – how the hell do you end up accidentally having healthy pregnancies when I don't after assiduous planning, expensive ovulation kits, and giving up caffeine, alcohol, and my sanity?

• I hate hearing your excitement about meeting your baby, bringing your baby home, and doing all the things I will never get to do with my first pregnancy—or maybe ever.

Exercise: How About Some Compassion with that Haterade?

This exercise is adapted from the wonderful Dr. Kristin Neff, researcher, writer, and all-around self-compassion guru.[30] Write a compassionate letter to yourself—yes, even when you're feeling your most hateful and dark (which might be the best time for it). I found this exercise so helpful, and have shared the letter I wrote below.

Part 1: Begin by writing about the specific situation or triggers that caused you to feel inadequate or bad about yourself. What emotions come up for you when you think about this aspect of yourself? Try to just feel your emotions exactly as they are – no more, no less – and then write about them.

Part 2: Now think about an imaginary friend who is unconditionally loving, accepting, kind, and compassionate. Imagine that this friend can see all your strengths and all your weaknesses, including the aspect of yourself you have just been writing about. Reflect upon what this friend feels towards you, and how you are loved and accepted exactly as you are, with all your very human imperfections. This friend recognizes the limits of human

---

[30] Neff, Kristin D, "Self-Compassion," in *Handbook of Individual Differences in Social Behavior* ed. Mark R. Leary and Rich H. Hoyle (New York: The Guilford Press, 2009): 561-573.

nature and is kind and forgiving towards you. In his/her great wisdom, this friend understands your life history and the millions of things that have happened to create you as you are in this moment. Your particular inadequacy is connected to so many things you didn't necessarily choose: your genes, your family history, your life circumstances – all of which are outside of your control.

Now, write a letter to yourself from the perspective of this imaginary friend – focusing on the perceived inadequacy you tend to judge yourself for. What would this friend say to you about your "flaw" from the perspective of unlimited compassion? How would this friend convey the deep compassion he/she feels for you, especially for the pain you feel when you judge yourself so harshly? What would this friend write in order to remind you that you are only human, that all people have both strengths and weaknesses? And if you think this friend would suggest possible changes you should make, how would these suggestions embody feelings of unconditional understanding and compassion?

As you write to yourself from the perspective of this imaginary friend, try to infuse your letter with a strong sense of his/her acceptance, kindness, caring, and desire for your health and happiness.

Part 3: After writing the letter, put it down for a little while. Then come back and read it again, really letting the words sink in. Feel the compassion as it pours into you, soothing and comforting you like a cool breeze on a hot day. Love, connection, and acceptance are your birthright. To claim them you need only look within yourself.

Here's what this exercise looked like for me:

Part 1: I started to feel bad about myself when I even imagined telling my friends that I would not be able to plan their baby shower. I felt guilty and weak and wondered why

I was not able to push my own feelings to the side to focus on what was such a huge and joyous event in their lives. I also felt sad, hopeless, and disconnected when I was at my friends' baby shower and I saw their other friends reaching towards my friends' pregnant bellies with wonder and excitement. I realized I had never once touched their pregnant bellies after my miscarriage and was immediately filled with disappointment, grief, and shame.

Part II: Dear Sunita, I can hear how much pain you have been in. I know it hurts to not be there for your friends in the way you want to and I know you wish you had this superhuman ability to push your emotions and the last few months aside and just pretend that everything is okay. I want you to know that it is okay that you are not okay. You have been through loss, pain, and trauma in the last few months. I know there have been times you have struggled to make it through the day, through work, through conversations with friends, and that's okay because you have been through so much.

You can be excited for your friends and still feel grief and loss for yourself. It's so absolutely human and natural to dread going to an event that is baby-centered when I know it's the last thing you want to think about, and that's okay. It's okay that you wish you could put the rest of the world on pause for a little while longer until you have some more time to grieve. It's okay that you dread going to that party, that you aren't as excited for your friends as you wish you could be, and it's okay if you go and just make it through the party because that is a lot right now. What I wish for you is that you offer yourself some grace, some compassion, and that you can see how strong you are. I wish that anytime you feel those feelings of sadness, anger, or disappointment come up when you see a pregnant person or anything baby-related that you can acknowledge those feelings and let yourself just notice them without fighting them, without judging them, and then you can tell yourself like I'm telling you know: It's okay to feel that way. There is no right way to feel after a loss. It's okay that you are not okay right now.

Love,

Sunita

(Also, Alex, who was the compassionate friend I was picturing.)

Chapter 10
MOVING FORWARD, NOT MOVING ON

#Goals for Pregnancy after Miscarriage

January is such a fun month to be a therapist. All my clients are coming in with that new-year energy, ready to do the work and get things moving. Also, I get to pull out one of my favorite catch phrases – "New Year, New Me!" – and gleefully announce it to whoever is around regardless of the context or ongoing conversations. People love it. January is the season for goal-setting, and whenever I help my clients in developing their goals for the new year, I always encourage them to begin by reflecting on their last year. I ask them to consider what were some big wins for them and why, and what were some disappointments, some challenges, and what have you learned from them?

This same kind of intentional reflection proved very helpful shortly after my first miscarriage, as the idea of facing pregnancy again was very daunting. Additionally, research suggests that women who have experienced previous pregnancy loss may be at further risk for developing psychiatric disorders in subsequent pregnancies.[31] Thus, a few months after my first miscarriage, I decided I wanted to do this exercise for myself (it just happened to be January – New Year, New Me!) to reflect on my experience of pregnancy and what I loved and what I wanted to do differently.

---

[31]   Giannandrea, S.   A., Cerulli, C., Anson, E.,   & Chaudron, L. H., "Increased Risk for Postpartum Psychiatric Disorders Among Women with Past Pregnancy Loss," Journal of Women's Health no. 22 (2013): 760–768.

Wins/What I would want to do again:

- Continuing to work out as I did pre-pregnancy (lower impact, but same frequency)
- Sharing the news with my family and friends (that may be a shocker for some, but their support was invaluable after the miscarriage)
- Making plans with Michael (even if those plans did not come to fruition, dreaming with my Michael about our future is something I will never regret)
- Eating more (correction, any) fruits and vegetables (I could go a whole week without ingesting a fruit or vegetable pre-pregnancy)
- Switching doctors and advocating for myself when I did not feel I was getting all the information I needed

What I do not want to repeat:

- Googling incessantly
- Fighting my feelings
- Putting things in my life on hold because I was pregnant
- Taking multiple pregnancy tests

This latter list is worth exploring because I know from experience that while these behaviors are not unusual, they can be so destructive. So, let's take them one at a time. First, I think we can all agree that Googling everything and anything under the sun is almost never helpful. Yes, it is important to stay informed and educated so that you can make the best decisions and advocate for yourself accordingly. But there is a fine line between being knowledgeable and driving yourself crazy with the contradicting information you find on the web. I will say with full transparency that I crossed this line multiple times. I was so far past it I couldn't even see it! As many of you know who have gone down the Googling rabbit hole before, with any question you have you can often find information that supports both a yea or a nay. Does lower back pain mean I'm having a miscarriage? This site says yes while that site says no. The wide range of information provided is not surprising given the broad spectrum of pregnancy symptoms women experience. For some, lower back pain could indicate a miscarriage while for others it's just a normal part of pregnancy. It's all so maddeningly random!

Second, I don't want to fight against my feelings. This is a point I've made in previous chapters, but it's so important it bears repeating. It's so normal that we will experience a range of uncomfortable emotions in both pregnancy and following a miscarriage, including sadness, shame, grief, anxiety, and maybe some hate thrown in there. Those feelings are hard enough to sit with without adding the extra burden of fighting against them or getting upset with ourselves for having those thoughts in the first place. With my first pregnancy, particularly, I tried so hard to fight against my anxiety. I would either try to dismiss it or berate myself for being so irrational. Not helpful!! Stop kicking the puppy (see Chapter 9). Or after my first miscarriage, I was upset with myself for being so upset about my miscarriage. See the dilemma there? Let's not compound our pain, dear readers.

Third, putting things in my life on hold because I was pregnant. Again, I did this more during my first pregnancy than my second pregnancy. You live and you learn, right? The reality is there are certain things you have to put on hold during pregnancy, including drinking, maybe learning a new sport, or making huge lifestyle changes because you are literally in the middle of one! I think I took this to a little bit of an extreme with my first pregnancy. I'm someone who thrives on being active and engaging in new learning, whether that's learning to skateboard or becoming familiar with a new therapeutic approach.

However, when I was pregnant my thoughts often went like this: "Ooh that couples therapy training event looks awesome, but hmmm it's in October. I'll be seven months pregnant then. Do I really want to go to an event in Chicago? Probably not, best to wait till next year." Or when the weather started to get really nice and I automatically thought about biking again, that thought evaporated in a millisecond, replaced by "But what if I fall? Best to not take any chances and keep doing my pregnancy-safe YouTube exercise videos." I imagine many women learn after their first or second pregnancy that you can keep living your life even when you are pregnant, and you should! You are still a person with a life and passions and these passions still deserve nourishment during pregnancy and during motherhood.

Fourth, and this one is a no-brainer, I do not want to take multiple—and I mean multiple— pregnancy tests. For one thing, those tests are damn expensive! Secondly, and really this is the reason that counts, I took multiple pregnancy tests during both of my pregnancies and every single one of them was a strong positive and yet here I am, two miscarriages later. Hate to be the downer here, but those tests offer no confirmation of a healthy pregnancy and just serve to give your anxiety more airtime.

Let's consider an example that happened to me not too long ago to further illustrate this point. My nephews, whom I love, came to visit us. One of them threw a tantrum-to-end-all-tantrums anytime we got in the car because he much preferred to play with my phone. Well-versed in the psychology of operant conditioning (i.e., the reinforcement and shaping of behaviors), you can imagine what I did next. I gave that child my phone real quick. Now, this immediately gave me some blessed relief, but I had started a vicious cycle because the next time we got in the car, my nephew not only wanted my phone again, he expected it, and I gave it to him again to stop his mounting tantrum. See what happened there? Eventually, I decided I needed to end this behavior and set a responsible example for my nephew – also, I just really got bored without my phone. So, instead of responding to his tantrum by giving in, I said nope, I need to hold on to this, but why don't you look outside and count how many red cars you see passing by? That game is as boring as it sounds, and my nephew protested and whined and it wasn't pleasant for anyone, but eventually he subsided. And y'all the next time we got in the car, no tantrum! My phone was all mine.

Essentially, the more we give in to our anxiety by engaging in avoidance or numbing behaviors, the more danger we are in of letting that anxiety build and build until it becomes a loud, angry monster that has a death grip on your phone. Similarly, the more we attempt to alleviate our anxiety with taking multiple pregnancy tests, the more we become dependent on that stimulus for short-term relief. We create a cycle of anxiety-pregnancy test-short-term relief-mounting anxiety, again and again until our next "fix." Instead, what if when that anxiety came, we sat with it, maybe we even leaned into the discomfort, gave it compassion, and let it be without trying to fix it.

"Yeah that sounds great, but how the hell do I do that?" That's often the response I get from clients when sharing this concept because it sounds counterintuitive to ask someone to move towards their pain instead away from it. As this is an ACT-based concept, I will use one my favorite ACT metaphors to describe this further: the Chinese Finger Trap. Dr. Brian Thompson, director of the Portland Psychotherapy Anxiety Clinic, explains the origins of this metaphor in his article, "Chinese Finger Traps: What a Novelty Item Can Teach Us About Acceptance."[32] Y'all

---

[32] Thompson, Brian, "Chinese Finger Traps: What a Novelty Item Can Teach Us About Acceptance," accessed June 22, 2019,

remember those (usually cheap) woven bamboo tubes where you would stick your index fingers in either end, and when you try to pull them out, the tube constricts, trapping your fingers. When you push your fingers inward, it causes them to loosen. Struggling against our pain by trying to avoid it is like trying to get out of a finger trap by pulling your fingers out with all your might. We always remain stuck.

When we try to get away from pain such as the anxiety or loss following miscarriage, the pain may tighten up on us, like the finger traps. Unfortunately, sometimes it's just this struggle to change what we are feeling that can make things worse, not better. Our lens become restricted to narrowly focusing on avoiding pain. We tell stories about it, and analyze it, and justify it, and explain it, and all we get for all that work is more, not less, pain. But when we lean into our discomfort, as when we gently press our index fingers into the finger trap, we create some space.

This part is important enough that I'll repeat it, y'all, this time directly from Thompson's article: "Leaning into discomfort doesn't free you—you're still in the trap—but you gain some wiggle room. A desire to pull away is natural—it tends to be our default—but it often gets us stuck."[33]

Alternatively, when we intentionally make space for our pain, we let go of the struggle. This allows us the freedom to move, to look around, and to choose what to do next.

P.S. If you ever need a reminder of this process, I highly recommend buying a cheap, bulk pack of Chinese finger traps online to play around with the next time you

---

https://portlandpsychotherapyclinic.com/2013/03/chinese-finger-traps-what-novelty-item-can-teach-us-about-acceptance/.
[33] Ibid.

notice yourself getting stuck.

The next step with this exercise is then to use these reflections to inform your goals for your next pregnancy. Here are the goals I came up with:

- Instead of Googling every concern that comes to mind, I will start a list on my phone of questions to ask my doctor.
- I will continue attending training conferences and engaging in activities that nourish me.
- I will allow myself to sit with a range of uncomfortable emotions without judging myself or trying to justify these emotions.
- I will make space for joy and excitement.

Now, a lot of my goals are related to my emotional health and mindset—an occupational hazard. For me, those were the biggest challenges during pregnancy. For others, their goals may center around wanting to share more with their partner or adopt healthier habits such as working out more consistently, meditating, or eating healthy. The world is your oyster, dream big!

Next, I encourage my clients to consider what specific behaviors/steps they would need to take to make these goals a reality. This is important. A lot of times we set goals without considering what support we need to really make them happen. Some tips here include:

- Get an accountability buddy. I love this. Ask your partner or another supportive person if they will help you reach this goal. If your goal is meditating, ask your accountability buddy if they would like to do this with you or if they are willing to check in with you at the end of the week to assess your progress.
- Make your goals realistic and specific. This is so vital! Define your goal into measurable components. For example, the goal of eating healthy is great, but

consider what you mean by this. Does this mean incorporating more fruits and vegetables into your diet or does it mean limiting the number of times you eat out? Or does it mean both? Also, make those goals realistic! The idea of never eating out would be impossible for me and would just set me up for failure (Chick-fil-A is a weekly occurrence in my family), but limiting take-out to two times a week is doable.

- Shape your environment to the goals you are setting. Want to start journaling? Put your journal somewhere accessible, such as on your nightstand so it's easily available. Anything you can do to streamline meeting your goals will make them more likely to happen.
- Find a system that works for you and stick to it. There are tons of amazing supports out there when it comes to goal-setting and planning, including apps like Habitca, great planners, reminders on your phone, and good old-fashioned to-do lists. Identify what system will be most helpful for you and make it happen!

Last, and this one is a game-changer, ask yourself what feelings, experiences, and thoughts are you willing to endure to reach your goal. My mind was blown the first time I read this question. Here's why: often we set a goal, we make a great plan to follow through, we put the right supports and systems in place—and then we are confronted by a barrier. This barrier can take many forms. It can be physical discomfort: waking up early to journal makes me a little sleepier in the mornings. It can be emotional discomfort: going to therapy has brought up some painful thoughts and feelings that I didn't expect. Maybe the barriers come from outside. I often caution my clients that some of the great, healthy changes they are making may result in some resistance from the people in their life. As I spend more time at the gym, my partner gets frustrated that I'm not as available as I used to be. Each of these barriers can be difficult, painful, and sometimes can become so uncomfortable that they stop us from moving forward on our goals. Thus, I want us to pause now and consider, what are we willing to endure to reach the goals we have set?

Here is what I am willing to endure to have a healthy pregnancy and a baby: I am willing to endure anxiety, so much anxiety. I know if I got pregnant again, I would be so anxious about the possibility of having another miscarriage. I am willing to endure the fear that I would experience another physical and emotional trauma. I am willing to endure the physical discomfort of pregnancy. I am willing to make changes in my lifestyle to support the health of myself and my pregnancy.

I want to add an important caveat here. It's important to also consider what you are *not* willing to endure for your goals. Maybe you are at a point that you would like to have kids and would like to get pregnant, but right now the idea of being confronted with that much anxiety and fear is not an option. Please hear me when I say that this is OKAY. We can want things so dearly AND know that we are not willing, wanting, or able to endure all the discomfort and pain that come with those things. It takes so much bravery and courage to acknowledge this and I hope you can feel the care I am sending you as you consider what those limits are for you.

Choosing Hope

The idea of being hopeful after a miscarriage or possibly multiple miscarriages seems impossible. Believe me, I know. We often distance ourselves from hope as a self-protective measure. We think "If I have no expectations, no hopes, then I will be less disappointed, less impacted by whatever happens." Sorry, but I'm going to have to call bullshit on that idea, speaking from both personal experience and from knowledge backed by research.

Let's start with the personal. With my first pregnancy, I felt so anxious because of the merry-go-round, never-ending appointments that left me with more questions and uncertainty than answers. I coped with this uncertainty by tamping down my feelings of hope and excitement for our baby. Anytime a little fragment of hope would emerge, such as daydreaming about names or what our baby would look like, I would savagely crush that thought and instead distract myself with work, television, or whatever was engaging enough to help me forget about the beautiful dreams I had for our baby.

The effects of not allowing myself to hope were internal conflict and unease, anxiety, and sadness – all the things I was trying to avoid by not allowing myself to hope. See how that works? Essentially, when we try to protect ourselves by not getting our hopes up, we then go on to experience all the painful feelings we were actually trying to avoid. Stupid self-fulfilling prophecy.

Let's get into some of the research. Brené Brown, a psychologist who has completed multiple studies on vulnerability, describes the idea of "foreboding joy." Foreboding joy refers to the tendency we have in moments of intense joy to turn towards fear, catastrophizing, or anxiety. Brown argues that experiencing joy takes vulnerability because it means that we need to have the courage to let our defenses down enough to feel joy.[34] I found myself experiencing numerous moments of foreboding joy in my first pregnancy when I would have an instance of happiness or excitement for our growing baby and then this hope would quickly be squashed as I worried

---

[34] Brown, Brené, Dare to Lead: Brave Work. Tough Conversations. Whole Hearts (New York: Random House, 2018).

about all the what-ifs. Instead of joy, I moved to considering how would I handle it if I experienced the worst-case scenario. What if I were told that I was having a miscarriage? I must have rehearsed that scenario hundreds of times. I let myself imagine all the painful feelings I would experience, I considered who I would have to tell, how I would handle work, and imagined again and again what that moment and subsequent days would be like, all in the futile hope that somehow by rehearsing this terrifying scenario enough, I would be prepared and somehow protected from the devastation that news would bring. I'm guessing you already know the punch-line here. The moment I heard we were having a miscarriage, I was shocked, surprised, and completely bowled over by my devastation. All my rehearsals of this event went out the window. I'm sorry to say, there is no level of mental or physical preparation that can prepare you or protect you from the pain and grief of having a miscarriage.

Now, let's consider another option. In my second pregnancy, I was again very anxious for the first month and still rarely allowed myself to hope, but after we had a first successful ultrasound and got to hear our baby's heartbeat, I let my hope fly like a stallion on the tracks. I gave in to all the dreaming and imagining, starting conversations with Michael about baby shower ideas and nursery ideas, and you should have seen my baby Pinterest boards. They were magnificent. Now, there were still moments of anxiety and worry, and in those moments, I would name what was happening. "Ah, it's my old friend, foreboding joy. That's okay, I don't need you right now. I'm going to enjoy this moment." And I did! I let myself fully lean into the hope and the excitement and the joy of pregnancy and early parenthood.

And then we found out we were having another miscarriage. Our hopes were certainly dashed then, and yet, as I reflect back, those few weeks when I let myself hope were so much happier, freer, and more enjoyable than the months I intentionally worked to tamp down my hopes. Brown suggests that allowing yourself to have hope and experience joy prepares you for grief and pain. I think of it like an emotional bank account. Allowing myself to experience hope, joy, and excitement were weighty deposits in my bank account, and the grief and loss I experienced were significant withdrawals. The only reason I didn't go completely bankrupt was from the emotional deposits I allowed myself to make.

Let me say it again, that whole idea of not getting your hopes up to make coping with potential loss easier to deal with is complete bullshit. Not getting your hopes up is what causes pain and stops you from experiencing joy. Even though my hopes have not been realized (yet), I am so appreciative of the few weeks my husband and I had to be hopeful, joyful, and happy together, and I wouldn't take them back for the world. What I would take back if I had that crystal ball (along with my hair style in middle school and not getting braces until adulthood) was the many times I did not give myself permission to hope because I was afraid it would make any future losses more painful.

I want to add a caveat here. In the hours and days immediately following our second miscarriage, I did not have this perspective. I did not think "Wow, I'm so glad we had that time to be hopeful and dream together" as I was completing my pre-op for my second D&C. Instead, I was pissed, disappointed, and devastated, and in my grief, I momentarily resented that I allowed myself to hope. How foolish of me. I will know better next time. And I do know better, after allowing myself more time to process and grieve, I can unequivocally say that hope is always the better choice and that if and when I get pregnant again, I will choose hope every single time.

One Destination, Many Paths

After my first miscarriage, I had no doubts about trying to get pregnant again and was sure that I would become a mother eventually. As I write this now, after experiencing my second miscarriage, I'm not so sure. As many of us who have traversed the pregnancy loss and fertility journey know, there are many unknowns on this path. At this point, Michael and I have started getting testing done to hopefully get some answers about what has caused our miscarriages and what our path to parenthood would look like if we so choose it. And that's what I want to explore here: our choices.

Shortly after my second miscarriage, I came across the previously mentioned and excellent "Miracles Happen Fertility Podcast" by Dr. Maria Rothenburger, which discusses the trials and tribulations of the fertility journey. One episode in particular really resonated with me. It was called "The Joy of Infertility. Wait. What?" I remember selecting that episode with hesitation, wondering what kind of Pandora's box I was about to open. The episode said that by definition, fertility refers to richness, fruitfulness, and generativity. And while we often limit this concept to the ability to conceive children, it can mean so much more. Having a fertile life can mean creating a life that has meaning, worth, and richness outside of children.[35]

Michael and I had many discussions about what fertility in our life could entail. We considered what already makes our life rich, including travel, learning new sports, spending time with family, and volunteering. We discussed that with the financial and logistical freedom of living child-

---

[35] Rothenburger, M. (2017-2019). Miracles Happen Fertility Podcast. Retrieved from https://podcasts.apple.com/us/podcast/mhfp-004-the-joy-of-infertility-wait-what/id1235974516?i=1000410984293.

free, our lived definition of fertility could continue to evolve. When we once daydreamed about the child we would have and the family we would grow, we began to daydream about a completely different kind of life. The landscape of each of these dreams was drastically different. However, I know with certainty that each would be filled with such joy, love, adventure, and fertility.

My intention here is not to advocate for any specific dream, but rather to share that the path to living a fertile life is not limited to one road. Additionally, I believe it is so important to take ownership of what path we take. It can feel like control or agency is taken from you after a miscarriage. You experience a painful emotional and physical trauma without any say in the matter. Thus, it is so important to acknowledge and hold onto the power you do have in your life following pregnancy loss. I was not able to predict or prevent either of my miscarriages, but I do have a say in choosing what path I take moving forward. Maybe I will try to get pregnant again. I will pursue fertility treatments and have a child that I will raise in the suburbs. We will take family vacations to national parks and my nephews will have cousins to grow up with. Or maybe I won't and Michael and I will move to the heart of downtown Houston and will split our time between our work and travelling the world. If you ask me, both options sound pretty damn good.

An Ode to Holland

As we end our journey together, I want to share with y'all a short essay I have always connected with. I came across it again after my second miscarriage and its meaning never felt truer:

> When you're going to have a baby, it's like you're planning a vacation to Italy. You're all excited. You

get a whole bunch of guidebooks, you learn a few phrases so you can get around, and then it comes time to pack your bags and head for the airport. Only when you land, the stewardess says, 'WELCOME TO HOLLAND." You look at one another in disbelief and shock, saying, "HOLLAND? WHAT ARE YOU TALKING ABOUT? I SIGNED UP FOR ITALY." But they explain that there's been a change of plan, that you've landed in Holland and there you must stay. "BUT I DON'T KNOW ANYTHING ABOUT HOLLAND!" you say. 'I DON'T WANT TO STAY!" But stay you do.

You go out and buy some new guidebooks, you learn some new phrases, and you meet people you never knew existed. The important thing is that you are not in a bad place filled with despair. You're simply in a different place than you had planned. It's slower paced than Italy, less flashy than Italy, but after you've been there a little while and you have a chance to catch your breath, you begin to discover that Holland has windmills. Holland has tulips. Holland has Rembrandts.

But everyone else you know is busy coming and going from Italy. They're all bragging about what a great time they had there, and for the rest of your life, you'll say, "YES, THAT'S WHAT I HAD PLANNED." The pain of that will never go away. You have to accept that pain, because the loss of that dream, the loss of that plan, is a very, very significant loss. But if you spend your life mourning the fact that you didn't get to go to Italy, you will never be free to enjoy the very special, the very lovely things about Holland.[36]

---

[36] Kingsley, E. P., "Welcome to Holland," (1987) accessed June 29,

Maybe you are in Holland or maybe you have found your way to Italy. Wherever you go, find the beauty in the place, find the beauty in yourself, and send me a postcard because I would love to hear all about the amazing life you have created.

2019, https://www.pdx.edu/students-with-children/sites/www.pdx.edu.students-with-children/files/Welcome%20to%20Holland.pdf.

Afterword

ONE LAST THING BEFORE WE GO

Dear readers, I so appreciate you taking this journey with me. As I mentioned at the beginning of this book, I'm sorry you have a reason to pick up *The Miscarriage Map*. Yet I hope you have gained something from our time together. Whether you are sipping the pregnancy/baby-hater-ade, the shame cocktail, or the grief gimlet, I want you to know you are not alone. I hope you have laughed alongside me and have felt seen and understood. I hope you know that when you are completely lacking in direction, there are steps you can take when you're ready. Last, I hope you have gained or reaffirmed the knowledge that you deserve all the care in the world from those around you and especially from yourself. Sending all the care in the world to you, dear readers.

D0369725